an Book

be re ... post, telephone,
m ... to re' m this

SUSTAINABLE
RURAL TOURISM

Opportunities for local action

Distributed by:
Countryside Commission Postal Sales
PO Box 124
Walgrave
Northampton NN6 9TL
Telephone: 01604 781848

© Countryside Commission 1995
CCP 483
ISBN 0 86170 464 9
Price £18.00

CONTENTS

	Page
Foreword	2
Introduction	3
Background	3
How to use this report	3
1. Setting the scene	4
Rural tourism and sustainability	4
Lessons from the case study projects	10
2. Local action for sustainable tourism	13
Making projects effective	13
Improving resource management and access	16
Marketing sustainable tourism	22
Managing traffic and transport	26
Involving the local community	31
Increasing local benefit	34
Changing visitor attitudes and behaviour	39
Influencing tourism enterprises	43
3. The case study projects	47
Project Explore, Cornwall	48
Devon and Cornwall Rail Partnership	51
Purbeck Heritage Committee, Dorset	54
Dartmoor Area Tourism Initiative	57
Peak Tourism Partnership	61
Surrey Hills Visitor Project	64
Wiltshire Downs Project	67
Tarka Project, Devon	70
North Pennines Tourism Partnership	74
South Somerset District Council	77
Lake District Traffic Management Initiative	80
South Devon Green Tourism Initiative	84
Settle and Carlisle Railway Development Company	87
Norfolk Coast Project	90
Nightingale Project, Kent	94
Case study project contacts	97
Acknowledgements	97

Recycled paper

FOREWORD

This report is for all those involved in developing, managing or marketing tourism in the countryside. It translates the concept of 'sustainability' in rural tourism into practical experience of what can be done on the ground. It draws lessons from recent case study projects, covering both strategic considerations of interest to policy makers and guidance to those working in the field.

Sustainable tourism — that is tourism which can sustain local economies without damaging the environment on which it depends — was widely debated when Government set up the Tourism and the Environment Task Force in 1990. The Task Force examined 'the scale and nature of the problems caused by visitor numbers .... and the environmental and other benefits which tourism brings' to historic towns, heritage sites and the countryside, and drew up guidance.

Maintaining The Balance, the Task Force report published in 1991, set out seven principles, which have now been widely adopted. It recognised that tourism and the environment should be seen as interdependent, each potentially of benefit to the other if properly managed. It also recommended that the tourist boards and other agencies should set up a series of pilot projects, applying potential solutions to local problems.

This present report summarises what has been learnt from a wide range of such initiatives, many of which have been actively encouraged and part-funded by the countryside agencies and the tourist boards. Written for the Countryside Commission, Department of National Heritage, English Tourist Board and the Rural Development Commission by The Tourism Company, it provides invaluable guidance on how rural tourism should be sustained. We trust you will find its advice of value.

Lord Inglewood
Minister for Tourism, Department of National Heritage

Richard Simmonds
Chairman, Countryside Commission

Adele Biss
Chairman, English Tourist Board

Lord Shuttleworth
Chairman, Rural Development Commission

Background

This advisory report examines sustainable tourism in the countryside. It assesses how it can be put into practice at a local level.

Sustainable tourism is a relatively new concept. It embraces the idea of striking a balance between the needs of the visitor, the environment and local communities. It is about encouraging an approach to tourism that can be maintained in the long term without degrading the environment in which it takes place. This is part of an emerging consensus about the need to embrace sustainable development as a way to safeguard future prosperity and well being.

The starting point for this report is the experience of a number of local projects. It is primarily a guide to the opportunities for local action rather than a comprehensive review of sustainable tourism. This report does not seek to address wider policy issues about the scale and nature of tourism and leisure development and activity in the countryside. However, it does state a number of strategic issues relating both to the practice of sustainable tourism and the organisation of local area projects.

Although based on examples in England, the findings will be of interest to practitioners throughout the UK and in other European countries, who have to address similar problems.

How to use this report

This report falls into three chapters — each chapter can be read independently and is treated rather differently.

- **Setting the scene** — this chapter looks at the subject in strategic and policy terms. It examines what is meant by sustainable rural tourism, and places it in the context of the Task Force report and emerging Government policy on sustainable tourism. It draws general lessons from the case study projects.
- **Local action for sustainable tourism** — this chapter takes a more practical view. It draws on the experience of the local projects to show how people have tried to put sustainable tourism into practice in some rural areas. It looks in detail at the range of tools and techniques available and discusses the pitfalls and the potential of these initiatives. It offers detailed examples of practice, drawn from the case study projects.
- **The case study projects** — this chapter looks at the experience of 15 significant projects. It examines how each project came about, its objectives, working arrangements, funding and achievements. It includes an evaluation of each project and draws out some general lessons and pointers. This section is perhaps best used as a source of reference.

At known 'beauty spots' visitor pressures can be intense at certain times. © Peak National Park.

Rural tourism and sustainability

Sustainable tourism is a term which crops up with increasing frequency and arouses a lot of interest as well as a degree of scepticism. Is this a way forward for rural tourism or is it pie in the sky? The debate is not helped by the lack of clarity about what the term actually means in practice.

This first chapter:

- considers the context of rural tourism and sustainable tourism in England;
- identifies some principles for sustainable rural tourism and what they mean in practice;
- draws some conclusions about the relevance and impact of sustainable rural tourism.

We then go on to look at the experience of the case-study projects which have provided the raw material for this advisory report; and evaluate their achievements and lessons to be learned from them.

Rural tourism

By rural tourism, we simply mean visitor activity in rural areas, including inland and coastal locations, open countryside and villages and small towns. We include both day trips and overnight stays in our definition of rural tourism, and use the term visitor to refer to anyone making such visits.

Rural tourism is not a discrete activity divorced from other forms of leisure activity. Visitors on holiday in rural areas may spend some of their time visiting towns or resorts. This relationship between tourism in rural areas and other places is important, and holds part of the answer to addressing the problems.

The countryside is an important resource for tourism in the UK, attracting a quarter of all domestic holiday nights and a third of all day trips. In round figures this means that each year British people take some 10 million holidays and spend some 45 million nights in the English countryside as well as making over 1,000 million day visits. Up to a half of England's 20 million overseas visitors also visit the countryside while they are in England and place a high value on its attractiveness.

The Rural Development Commission estimates that tourism is worth at least £8 billion a year to England's rural areas, and supports some 400,000 jobs. Tourism is therefore a very significant part of the rural economy, indeed in some areas it is the largest single sector of employment.

With the decline in agriculture and other sectors of employment, many rural areas are looking to tourism to make an even greater contribution in the future. Tourism can also bring social and environmental benefits to the local community through the support of local services and by generating new uses for redundant buildings.

Rural tourism can also bring costs, through intrusive development, traffic congestion, erosion and disturbance to wildlife and local people. However, such problems are often highly localised and seasonal in nature.

The House of Commons Environment Committee, in their recent report *The Environmental Impact of Leisure Activities*, concluded that leisure and tourism do not cause widespread ecological damage to the countryside; but that there are important issues to address concerning transport, problems in specific areas, and cultural conflicts, the latter being often more significant than the physical problems.

The number of visitors to the countryside has been more or less static over the past decade, although there have undoubtedly been changes in the pattern and incidence of use. However, trends such as the continuing growth in car ownership, rising affluence and population growth could well generate a greater volume of activity in the future. Patterns of recreation also change over time and bring new pressures with them, such as the growth in mountain biking and adventure sports.

So, there is growing recognition of the important contribution that tourism can make to the rural economy and a desire to develop this further. On the other hand, there is mounting concern about the impact of tourism on the character of the countryside and the people who live there. These concerns are prompting a search for better ways to manage and develop tourism in rural areas. That is why there is growing interest in sustainable tourism.

Additional income from visitors can keep village services viable.
© *Simon Warner/CC.*

Sustainable tourism

Sustainable tourism is about the relationship of visitors to the physical and to the social environment. It has been defined by the World Tourism Organisation as: 'Tourism which meets the needs of present tourists and host regions while protecting and enhancing opportunity for the future'.

Sustainable tourism has only become widely discussed in the UK within the last five years. Thinking on this subject has been developed from two strands — international concern about global environmental issues and local concerns about the impact of tourism on the environment and communities.

International concern about global environmental issues

In the late 1980s, concern about climate change, depletion of natural resources and pollution led to the concept of 'sustainable development'. This identified the need to take a long term view of the impact of our actions on the environment and the consequences for future generations.

The concept was endorsed at the Earth Summit in Rio in 1992. The UK Government then signed up to Agenda 21, committing itself to preparing strategies and action plans to put sustainable development into practice. In 1994 the Government published *Sustainable development – The UK strategy*. This has a chapter on leisure, which commits the Government to pursuing a sustainable approach, urges the statutory agencies to promote and develop good practice, asks local authorities to develop green strategies for tourism and recreation, and commends the approach to the private sector and the general public.

Most government agencies have now published statements on sustainable development. All local authorities are now drawing up Local Agenda 21 strategies to develop and coordinate action on sustainable development. Tourism and recreation strategies will increasingly be part of this.

Local concerns about the impact of tourism on the environment and on communities

Local concerns about the impact of tourism on the environment and on communities led to a string of policy initiatives within the UK. In 1989, the English Tourist Board and the Countryside Commission published their *Principles for tourism in the countryside*. This identified an approach to developing tourism in the countryside which would generate benefits to visitors and local communities without damaging the environment.

Most people simply enjoy just being in the countryside. ©Andy Tryner/CC.

Shortly after this the Government set up a Task Force on tourism and the environment. This reported in 1991. It recommended that the tourism industry and government should adopt seven principles for sustainable tourism (see box below); and that pilot projects should be established to explore and demonstrate practical techniques of visitor management.

The Task Force report sparked off a wave of interest in the subject and led to the publication of a series of advisory reports and policy statements as well as the establishment of a number of local projects designed to put theory into practice. Most of these were in rural areas. This report follows directly from this initiative, and is charged with evaluating and disseminating the experience of these projects.

Task Force principles for sustainable tourism

- The environment has an intrinsic value which outweighs its value as a tourism asset. Its enjoyment by future generations and its long term survival must not be prejudiced by short term considerations.
- Tourism should be recognised as a positive activity, with the potential to benefit the community and the place as well as the visitor.
- The relationship between tourism and the environment must be managed so that the environment is sustainable in the long term. Tourism must not be allowed to damage the resource, prejudice its future enjoyment or bring unacceptable impacts.
- Tourism activities and developments should respect the scale, nature and character of the place in which they are sited.
- In any location, harmony must be sought between the needs of the visitor, the place and the host community.
- In a dynamic world some change is inevitable and change can often be beneficial. Adaptation to change, however, should not be at the expense of any of these principles.
- The tourism industry, local authorities and environmental agencies all have a duty to respect the above principles and to work together to achieve their practical realisation.

Maintaining The Balance 1991.

Sustainable rural tourism — principles and practice

The concept of sustainable tourism is particularly relevant in rural areas, striving to maximise local benefit from tourism while minimising the effect of visitor pressure.

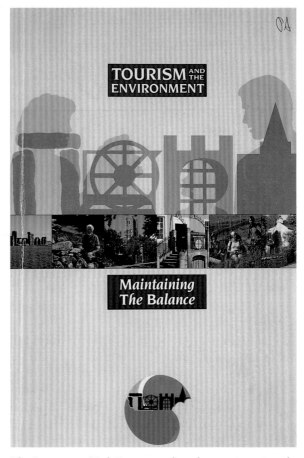

The Government Task Force report brought many issues into the open. © English Tourist Board.

Set out on the next page are some principles for sustainable rural tourism, based on the above background and on experience from the local projects studied.

The key idea, drawn from the Task Force, is that a harmony or balance should be sought between the needs of the **visitor**, the **place** (or local environment) and the **host community**. Sustainable rural tourism is about finding the right relationship between these elements in rural areas.

Villages provide a focus for rural tourism and the local economy. © Jeremy Haslam/CC.

In considering these relationships and balances, it is important to recognise the following points:

- The influences are two-way. Tourism can influence the environment and host communities, and vice versa.
- There are both positive and negative impacts in each direction. Tourism can benefit the environment as well as harm it. Environmental appreciation can enhance visitor enjoyment.
- The relationships are dynamic, not fixed. Sustainable tourism is about managing change in an acceptable way, rather than preserving things exactly as they are.

Rather than talking about minimising impact, therefore, we suggest that sustainable rural tourism should refer to 'sustaining' each element, through the influence of the other elements upon it.

In addition, tourism's impact on the **global environment** should be minimised.

From these points arise the following principles of sustainable rural tourism. Those involved in **tourism** should strive:

- **To minimise impact on the global environment:**
  - by avoiding pollution and the depletion of natural resources; and
  - by encouraging forms of tourism enterprise, operations and transport which are environmentally benign.
- **To sustain the local environment:**
  - by recognising limits to the capacity of different locations to receive more visitors,
  - by avoiding congestion, erosion and disturbance to wildlife, through better visitor management; and
  - by encouraging forms of tourism which sustain the character and diversity of the countryside and support its conservation:
    - directly, through restoration and maintenance of old buildings, landscapes, nature reserves, crafts and traditions etc and encouraging visitors to help fund conservation; and
    - indirectly, though increasing visitors' awareness of conservation issues.
- **To sustain the host community:**
  - by increasing the opportunity for rural areas to benefit economically from tourism, particularly encouraging those forms of tourism which retain visitor spending in local communities; and
  - by minimising nuisance and conflict from tourism in local communities, and involving local people in the planning and management of tourism in their areas.
- **To sustain the visitor:**
  - by recognising the visitor's right to enjoy and experience the countryside, and enabling access to it by all kinds of visitor where possible and appropriate; and

Increasing numbers of visitors have an interest in wildlife. © *John Robinson/ICCE.*

  - by providing visitors with a welcoming, meaningful and satisfying experience, and helping to increase their appreciation and understanding of the countryside.

These principles have implications for many aspects of tourism activity, including the kinds of tourism which should be encouraged, the messages to put over in marketing, the way the countryside is interpreted, and the way visitors and traffic are managed on the ground.

To show how these principles might be translated into practice we have drawn up a simple checklist (see next page) which could be used by local authorities and other interests seeking to develop a more sustainable approach to rural tourism. This is based on the experience gained from the projects examined. It should be seen as a starting point which needs further refinement. A not dissimilar list is given in the Environment Committee report *The Environmental Impact of Leisure Activities*.

Each of the elements in the checklist corresponds to a section in Chapter 2, where we explore in more detail how the principles can be turned into practice.

Sustainable rural tourism — a checklist for local authorities and other interests

ELEMENTS	AIMS	ACTIVITIES
1. Resource management	Protect and maintain local environmental quality	* Prepare visitor management plan * Take action to protect sensitive sites * Maintain and promote visitor routes * Record visitor numbers at key sites * Monitor sensitive sites * Assess environmental impact of proposed developments
2. Marketing	Influence scale and type of tourism in response to environmental and local factors	* Promote green messages to visitors * Avoid promotion of sensitive sites * Collaborate with local tourism operators * Collaborate with environmental agencies * Extend the season to spread impact and benefit * Monitor impact of marketing
3. Transport	Reduce the use and impact of cars	* Promote use of public transport * Improve services to meet needs of visitors * Introduce traffic management schemes for pressure points * Develop comprehensive area strategy * Monitor traffic volumes
4. Community	Involve local people in shaping tourism policy	* Set up community tourism forums * Support community based initiatives * Involve community in drawing up visitor management plans
5. Local benefit	Increase local economic contribution from tourism	* Promote local purchasing initiatives * Set up networks of local producers * Set up local heritage trusts * Assist local businesses to get more from tourism
6. Visitor welcome	Influence visitor behaviour to reduce negative impact and increase environmental awareness	* Raise awareness of conservation issues in print * Emphasise special character of area through imaginative interpretation * Increase contact between visitors and locals * Improve the welcome to visitors
7. Tourism industry	Reduce the environmental impact of the local tourism industry	* Promote use of the *Green Audit Kit* * Encourage adoption of environmental charters * Introduce environmental award schemes * Support environmental advice and training * Raise enterprises' awareness of their local environment

How relevant is sustainable tourism?

Based on our experience from the projects studied, we set out below some conclusions about the relevance and importance of sustainable tourism in rural areas.

- **Sustainable tourism is an approach, not a finite set of activities**. There is a tendency to equate sustainable tourism with a handful of low key activities in the countryside such as walking, cycling, or farm visits, which are often labelled as 'green tourism'. This is misguided and unhelpful. Sustainable tourism is wider than this, and should be seen as an approach which has implications for all kinds of rural tourism at all levels — national, regional, local — and on specific sites. It has implications for large as well as small developments; and for resorts and towns which surround rural areas and which might have a part to play in absorbing the pressure of visitors. Solutions will vary according to the nature and fragility of the rural area and the pressures involved, but the basic principles to be applied are the same.

- **It is a new name, not a new activity**. Many of the principles outlined above have been embraced within the town and country planning system, and are established practice in countryside management and rural economic development. The advent of the name 'sustainable tourism' simply marks a recognition of global environmental issues and a shift of emphasis towards an integrated approach to tourism in the countryside, whereby tourism is managed for the benefit of visitors, the environment and local communities.

- **It is a powerful approach which will gain in credibility**. The case study projects suggest that there is growing support and enthusiasm for sustainable tourism at a local level. Factors working in its favour include:
  - a high level of public interest in conservation and environmental issues;
  - growing public awareness of the need for control over issues such as traffic and pollution;
  - the emerging policy and legislative framework from local authorities, UK government and the European Union; and
  - increasing vociferousness of pressure groups and communities under pressure.

- **Sustainability cannot be achieved by local action alone**. The immediate problems often manifest themselves at a local level. Local action is undoubtedly required and can often be effective, but the pressures generally result from factors outside local control, such as levels of car ownership, social attitudes, growth in prosperity etc. Moreover, the ability of local agencies to take action often depends on external factors such as the resources available to them, the legislative and planning framework, transport policy, fiscal structures, and public attitudes in general. Sustainability can only become a reality if it is practised at all levels, and if local agencies are working within a framework which promotes it. This requires both a 'top-down' and a 'bottom-up' approach.

- **Visitor management can be effective given the resources**. Notwithstanding the above, the experience of the projects shows that in many cases visitor management can be effective in solving or at least ameliorating local problems. There is no widespread or immediate crisis resulting from visitor pressures in the countryside. There are some acute local problems, but most of these are amenable to management, given the will, imagination and necessary resources. We discuss some of the techniques available in Chapter 2. However, to repeat, effective local action requires resources and needs to be carried out within the context of national and regional policy towards sustainability.

- **Visitors may be receptive to the ideas of sustainable tourism**. One test of the relevance of rural sustainable tourism is the extent to which there is a market for it. Nationally, there is evidence that a significant proportion of the population is concerned about environmental matters and that this influences their purchasing patterns. However, there is little evidence as yet in the UK as to how much this concern has spilled over to tourism. The projects have shown that visitors are responding quite positively to local initiatives, such as supporting conservation or using public transport. However, it is not yet clear how far or how fast this can be pursued. In particular it would be helpful to know far more about how visitors feel about this, the degree of importance they place on environmental issues in their leisure time and the scope for influencing their behaviour.

- **A commitment to monitoring is essential**. Sustainable tourism is primarily about managing tourism to achieve wider social, economic and environmental objectives. Without any commitment to measuring impact on either a qualitative or quantitative basis, it is impossible to decide whether one is moving towards sustainable tourism or away from it. Sustainability implies a greater commitment to monitoring the impacts of policies and adjusting them in the light of results: we expand on this in Chapter 2.

Action to promote sustainable rural tourism

The concept of sustainable tourism is still very unfocused at present. This report is designed to clarify the concept and to link it to a framework of practical action to pursue on the ground.

Action is needed at a local and national level:

- **Local authorities have a fundamental role to play.** They can provide the continuity, long term perspective, political legitimacy and a holistic view. This does not mean that they should do it alone: they need to work in partnership with other interests. Partnership is a powerful tool for stimulating commitment and enthusiasm and getting things moving.

- **National agencies will continue to promote sustainable rural tourism, and to provide expertise.** The English Tourist Board and Regional Tourist Boards, the Countryside Commission and the Rural Development Commission have been active in developing and promoting this approach, often through joint initiatives. There may be need for further demonstration projects, but the prime emphasis will be the promotion of sustainable tourism amongst all those involved in tourism.

- **Sustainable tourism should be considered within the wider policies of Government.** Policies on roads, public transport, pollution, waste management and planning may all need to take account of it. Government has a key role to play in influencing public opinion, encouraging the participation of the tourism industry, and providing direction and support for local authorities.

- **The tourism industry must be brought on board.** There are promising signs that sections of the tourism industry are beginning to take environmental issues more seriously. Indeed in some projects, tourism operators have taken a leading role in working with local authorities and the local community. However, there is a considerable job yet to be done in persuading the industry that sustainable tourism offers the best way forward. This as an important task for the tourist boards and local authorities.

Lessons from the case study projects

The findings of this report are based on a review of 21 case study projects in the English countryside which were specifically set up to develop and promote sustainable tourism practices, or which had a strong element of sustainable tourism within their remit.

Case study projects:

- Birds of the Humber Trust
- Celebrate the Countryside, West Country
- Country Village Weekend Breaks, Herefordshire
- Dartmoor Area Tourism Initiative
- Devon and Cornwall Rail Partnership
- Lake District Traffic Management Initiative
- Nightingale Project, Kent
- Norfolk Coast Project
- North Pennines Tourism Partnership
- North York Moors Regional Routes
- Peak Tourism Partnership
- Project Explore, Cornwall
- Purbeck Heritage Committee, Dorset
- Settle and Carlisle Railway Development Company
- South Devon Green Tourism Initiative
- South Somerset District Council
- Surrey Hills Visitor Project
- Tarka Project, Devon
- The Big Apple, Herefordshire
- Wiltshire Downs Project
- Yorkshire Dales Food, Drink and Craft Trails

The nature of the case study projects

The projects covered by these case studies are by no means the only sustainable tourism initiatives that have been proceeding during this period.

Nearly all of the projects have been established in the past five years; were set up as fixed life projects; and are collaborative, involving partnerships between local authorities, regional and national agencies and other local interests.

Some are focused on small geographical areas within a single local authority. Others cover an entire sub-region and cross the boundaries of many authorities. Some attempt to pursue an integrated and comprehensive approach to sustainable tourism, while others focus on a particular theme or topic such as transport or marketing.

The projects are also quite varied in origin, and in the pattern of organisations taking the lead and participating. Thus some projects have a strong economic development focus, while others are more concerned with countryside management or tourism development.

Three of the projects were set up directly as a result of the Task Force report and were defined as national pilot projects, although others were established in the light of the interest generated by the report. Of the 21 projects, 16 were funded by the Countryside Commission, 11 by the English Tourist Board through the Regional Tourist Boards, and 8 by the Rural Development Commission. All involved local authority funding, and most also attracted funding from several other sources. Clearly the availability of funding from the national and regional agencies has been fundamental in establishing these projects and without it few would have been undertaken.

The 21 projects have attracted a total core funding of some £2.5m, of which 45 per cent came from national or regional agencies. This funding has paid for employment of project officers, and been used to pump-prime a range of initiatives. The projects have also had an impact in stimulating a significant amount of investment in work associated with their programmes which would not have taken place otherwise.

So, have these projects represented value for money, what have they achieved and what has been learned about sustainable tourism as a result?

Evaluating the case study projects

The sheer diversity of the studies and the fact that they were working to different briefs and objectives makes systematic evaluation or any quantitative assessment very difficult.

A detailed review of each project and the various initiatives undertaken is given in Chapters 2 and 3 of this report. We confine ourselves here to drawing some general conclusions about what the projects have achieved. This is presented under five headings:
• developing an approach to sustainable tourism;
• changing attitudes in the tourism industry;
• changing visitor behaviour;
• involving the local community; and
• improving the local environment.

Developing an approach to sustainable tourism

• **Increased support for sustainable tourism**. Despite differing approaches to sustainable tourism, the projects have all made explicit the link between tourism and the environment. There is now a much greater awareness of the principles of sustainable tourism within these areas. Support has been generated for tourism management, where before people were apathetic or even hostile to the very idea of tourism.

• **Improved working relationships**. The projects have made a significant impact in breaking down barriers and encouraging people to work together. This has brought people together from different disciplines and departments and also from different authorities and agencies. These partnerships have been made possible because the projects were seen as independent and have flourished even in the climate of the local government review. They have enabled log jams to be broken, resulted in a cross-fertilisation of ideas and liberated additional resources. This collaborative working seems set to continue in many places.

• **New approaches have been developed and tested**. The availability of project funding has given a measure of freedom to experiment and innovate, against a backdrop of constraints on public sector spending. This has helped in developing new ideas and approaches to sustainable tourism. Some of these are described in Chapter 2. This experience has not only been of value to the local area but has helped to stimulate and inform action elsewhere in the country. Some of these projects have developed a high profile and have been very influential in this respect.

Changing attitudes in the tourism industry

• **Useful inroads in a few areas**. Some projects have formed very productive relationships with the local tourism industry. They have raised awareness of environmental issues and responsibilities and have helped to establish groupings which will continue to develop and will take forward the ideas. Transport operators in particular have been enthusiastic participants. Owners and managers of small enterprises often have strong roots in the communities in which they are based, and are supportive of the ideas underlying sustainable tourism.

- **For most tourism businesses, sustainable tourism is not a priority**. The experience of working with the local tourism industry has been mixed. In rural areas the tourism industry largely consists of small, independent enterprises which are economically fragile, operate to a short time horizon and relate to their immediate locality. Business survival is the first priority, and sustainable tourism comes way down the list of their concerns. The recession has inevitably focused people's attention on survival. Raising awareness and building trust with the local tourism industry is a slow process, and is very dependent on personalities.

Changing visitor behaviour

- **Some visitors support sustainable tourism**. The projects have had some successes in this area. They have shown that some visitors at least are receptive to the ideas underlying sustainable tourism. They will support public transport initiatives, will make a contribution to conservation, and are enthusiastic about using new and properly planned facilities for enjoying the countryside.

- **The impact is still quite limited**. Nevertheless, and not surprisingly given the limited resources at their disposal and short timescale, the vast bulk of visitors have remained untouched by these projects. What is still not clear is the extent to which visitors in general are responsive to a green message and how best to influence them. Better monitoring of some of the initiatives would have helped towards providing an answer to these questions, but research at a national level is required.

Involving the local community

- **There is considerable enthusiasm for the projects among local people**. The level of interaction with local communities has varied according to the nature and scale of the project. Most of the projects have made efforts to inform and consult local communities. Many have had parish and town council representation on steering and working groups. Some of the projects have gone further, and have actively involved local community groups and other organisations in planning and pursuing the initiatives.

- **Consultation and involvement is not an easy road**. Where efforts have been made to involve the local community, it has proved to be a time consuming and sometimes difficult process. However, it has been educative for all concerned, and has helped to broaden perspectives. It has reduced if not eliminated conflict, and has generated a momentum and support for action that otherwise would not have existed. A key lesson is that the term 'community' covers a variety of different interest groups; and that friction within the community may be stronger than friction between the community and visitors.

Improving the local environment

- **Most projects will leave behind tangible benefits**. Some projects have resulted in physical improvements such as better car parking, tidying up of sites, and conservation projects. Other projects have helped to bring schemes forward, to change their emphasis or to develop a new strategy.

Conclusions

Taken together these projects have been useful, with some solid local achievements and some broader lessons from which others can learn. Many have acted as catalysts and have helped to change local attitudes to tourism. By being seen as separate from the existing bureaucracy and structures, project officers have often achieved more in terms of influencing opinion and winning support than they could have done as local authority officers.

Some projects might have achieved more if they had been less ambitious and more focused in their activities. Given that local involvement is a central tenet of sustainable tourism, it is to be expected that the projects have to some extent followed local priorities and interests. More attention might have been given to monitoring and to the winding up of the projects.

The next chapter looks in more detail at what the projects have done, how they have tried to put sustainable tourism into practice, and the lessons that can be learned as a result.

This chapter is concerned with examining how people have tried to put sustainable tourism into practice in some rural areas. It covers a broad spectrum of activities and initiatives — some aimed at the visitor, some aimed at local communities, some aimed at adapting and protecting the physical environment and some aimed at the local tourism industry.

We have grouped these activities into the following broad themes or topics:

- Making projects effective.
- Improving resource management and access.
- Marketing sustainable tourism.
- Managing traffic and transport.
- Involving the local community.
- Increasing local benefit.
- Changing visitor attitudes and behaviour.
- Influencing tourism enterprises.

The information and conclusions are drawn almost entirely from the 21 case study projects studied. As projects are not the only way to develop sustainable tourism, this is not, therefore, a definitive guide to all the tools and techniques available. It does, however, offer an overview of the range of techniques, an indication of how and where these have been put into practice, and an assessment of some of the benefits and the pitfalls.

Throughout this section, comments and conclusions are illustrated by a number of specific examples drawn from the case study projects. These are in boxes alongside the text; their purpose is to show how the various techniques have been used in practice. Additional information on 15 of the more comprehensive case study projects can be found in Chapter 3.

This section is mainly about what the projects have done to promote sustainable tourism, but there are also lessons to be drawn about what goes to make projects successful and effective. We begin, therefore, by summarising some lessons about project organisation and management.

Making projects effective

Five elements appear to have a significant impact on the effectiveness of projects. These are:

- Using project officers effectively.
- Defining the scope of the project.
- Setting up an appropriate organisational structure.
- Monitoring and measuring results.
- Winding up the project.

We discuss these and highlight some conclusions below.

Using project officers effectively

Most of the projects have appointed a project officer or manager to run the project on a day to day basis under the supervision of a steering group. Typically, staffing and administration have taken up 50–60 per cent of core funding: so, it is imperative to make the best use of project officers or other staff. The main reasons why projects have employed project officers (as opposed to using existing staff) is that there is rarely anyone available locally with either the experience or the time to take on the job. Moreover, it is often important that the project officer is seen to be independent and not linked to any one interest.

Projects have helped to break down barriers and involve local people. © Mark Boulton/ICCE.

The experience of the projects suggests that:

- The personality and skills of the project officer are very important in determining progress. It is a hard and testing job. Project officers have to be able to win respect. They need energy and resilience, must be open and tactful but also capable of being firm when necessary. It is worth taking some time and trouble in choosing and keeping a project officer, because changing project officers in mid-stream can be very disruptive in a short term project.
- Project officers are a valuable resource and need to be used effectively. Administrative support can help free them up for more important duties. Outside consultants have also been used effectively by some projects to facilitate and develop initiatives.
- Most project officers have found it useful to be involved in drawing up their own strategy and work programme. This helps to provide a sense of ownership and provides credibility with the steering group.
- To make the best use of the project officer, it is good to get as much in place as possible before the project formally starts. Some projects have used consultants to undertake studies or draw up general strategies, which have provided a useful context for the project officer to work within.

fining the scope of the ject

The projects have varied considerably in terms of the size of the area they have covered and the scope of their programme. The right approach will obviously depend to some extent on the objectives of the project. If the aim is to test some new and innovative ideas, then it is better to focus on, and be single minded about, those areas. If the aim is to encourage agencies and local interests to work more closely together, then the output may be less important than the process and a broader approach might be justified.

Nevertheless some general lessons can be drawn from the experience of the projects:

- Beware of being too ambitious. Almost all projects have tried to take on too many initiatives, given their limited resources. This is partly the responsibility of the funding bodies, who tend to encourage a wide range of objectives to match their different remits. Too many initiatives dissipate resources, so that the project officer spends a disproportionate amount of time simply chasing up progress.
- The larger the area, the more difficult it becomes to generate awareness of the project and to communicate with local interests. Where projects straddle many local authorities, it has proved more difficult to generate political support and involvement. Projects that have worked within one local authority area have found life much simpler.
- Beware of overlap and duplication between projects, which cause confusion. It is important to agree at the outset where the responsibilities of the different agencies and bodies lie, otherwise much of the impact of the project will be wasted.

Setting up an appropriate organisational structure

Almost all projects have some form of steering group to oversee the project, comprising representatives of the various sponsors. Some projects, have also set up working groups to shadow the steering group or to pursue specific initiatives. Whilst involving other interests in these projects is fundamental, there is a danger of creating an unwieldy and top-heavy structure that hinders communication and initiative.

The experience of the projects suggests the following conclusions:

- For most projects, there are considerable benefits in involving elected members in the steering group. Projects that have not done this have sometimes found it harder to generate support and to mobilise resources for implementation.

- Avoid having too many management groups; they are counter-productive and just add to bureaucracy and paperwork. Often the same people end up sitting on each group. An approach which has worked well in some projects is to have just one management group, and to establish smaller working groups as and when necessary; these groups are disbanded when they have served their purpose.
- An important role for representatives on steering and working groups is to spread the word about the project within their own organisations.

The projects varied between those which took direct action, largely through the project officer; and those which played more of an enabling role, in order to identify, coordinate, allocate and chase action to be carried out by others. Theoretically the enabling projects can achieve more and can ensure that the action is embedded in existing organisations at the end of the project; but this does depend on organisations showing consistent commitment. An action-orientated project can lead to swifter results in the short term.

It is probably best to seek a balance between both types of approach. For this the project needs:

- genuine working groups where action can be apportioned; and
- sufficient project funding to enable it to achieve some initial results and have some clout, but not so much that organisations see no need to take action themselves.

Monitoring and measuring results

There are three kinds of monitoring relevant to projects:

- keeping track of progress and budgets;
- measuring the impact of the initiatives undertaken;
- monitoring volumes of tourism and evidence of its impact on the environment over time.

Most projects have performed the first task well and have devised adequate reporting and budgeting systems. Setting up such systems is quite a task in itself. Time might have been saved by devising a standard package for all project officers to use.

Many projects have fallen down in measuring effectiveness of activities. The English Tourist Board devised a system of performance measures for the projects with which it was involved; but most found this too cumbersome and it was abandoned. There are various reasons why monitoring is poor:

- With pressure to get things happening on the ground, monitoring can seem like a diversion and waste of resources.
- Many initiatives have only just been established and it is too early to measure their impact; and
- It is difficult and relatively costly to measure the impact of small scale projects.

Monitoring needs to be well structured and objective. © Paul Davies.

Few projects have been involved with general monitoring of the impact of tourism. With hindsight, baseline surveys of visitors and sites might have helped some projects put their work in context. However, it is more realistic for projects to concentrate on specific monitoring of their own activities than to seek evidence of change from global measures on which they may have only a marginal influence.

Without any attempt to measure impact, it is very difficult to know what works and what doesn't. Pilot projects have a particular responsibility in this respect. Indeed there is an argument that if it is not possible to measure the impact of an initiative it should not be done in the first place.

There are some good examples of monitoring in the projects. The Devon and Cornwall Rail Project undertook a passenger survey and was able to measure increases in passenger loadings. The South Devon Green Tourism Initiative was able to measure the uptake of the Green Audit Kit and commissioned an independent assessment of it. The North Pennines project used a local college to undertake a survey of businesses to ascertain levels of awareness and contact with the project; and has also carried out visitor surveys to measure changes over the period. In South Somerset District Council, monitoring has been central to their whole approach to marketing, enabling them to adjust their work each year and to win additional resources for successful campaigns.

The experience shows that projects with effective monitoring have been in a much stronger position to argue for more resources and support.

Lessons from this are as follows:
- Build in time and resources for monitoring from the start.
- Avoid cumbersome procedures which are hard to maintain.

- Consider paying others to monitor initiatives; this ensures it gets done and is objective.
- Monitor all marketing work by keeping a clear record of enquiries and helping selected enterprises to track sources of bookings.
- Make use of modest visitor surveys, which can be simple to do and revealing, for instance in giving a reaction to information and interpretation.
- Obtain regular feedback from the tourism industry and local interests on their perception of the project and its effectiveness. In itself this helps communication.

Winding up the project

There is a danger that when a project comes to the end of its life it simply fizzles out leaving very little trace. This can mean that much of its impact is lost. Few of the projects have had a formal 'exit strategy' to deal with this, and most have had problems with the handover. In fact the final year of a project can be quite frenetic, as many initiatives only come to fruition towards the end of (say) a three year period.

The projects have approached this in a number of ways. A number of projects have been extended for a further term, such as Project Explore and Surrey Hills. In the case of the South Devon Green Tourism Initiative, national agencies have taken on the funding and adaptation of the Green Audit Kit as a national initiative. The Tarka project is working closely with the tourist industry to encourage them to take over and continue certain aspects of the project.

The lessons from this are as follows:
- An exit strategy should be considered at the outset of any project, rather than when the end is drawing near; and should be a condition of funding. However, it can be difficult to predict the outcome at the beginning, and it needs to be borne in mind that projects are dynamic and may change, so some flexibility is required.
- Efforts should be made to hand over successful initiatives to established agencies or private sector networks during the life of the project, while the project officer is there to assist.
- Some mechanism needs to be put in place to ensure that initiatives current at the end of the project are supported and followed through. There is a case for retaining the project officer for a period after the formal termination of the project to help with the transition.

Improving resource management and access

Good management of the countryside resource is fundamental for sustainable tourism. A balanced approach is needed, which enhances opportunities for rural tourism but which takes account of the ability of locations and individual sites to accommodate visitors.

The aims are to:

- reduce visitor impact on specific sites or areas of countryside;
- manage sites so they are better able to accommodate visitors, to the benefit of the environment and visitors themselves;
- channel visitors onto sites or routes with more capacity;
- manage potential conflict between different types of recreational user;
- increase opportunities for rural tourism based on appropriate countryside access;
- ensure that the nature and design of development is appropriate to the local rural environment; and
- benefit the local economy through sensitive development of countryside resources and sites as visitor attractions.

Most of the projects have been involved with resource management to some extent. A few have prepared or made an input to visitor management strategies, and some have undertaken site improvement or management work. Many projects have extended public access through the creation and marketing of walking and cycling routes and a few have been involved with horse riding. We discuss these approaches in more detail below.

Integrating rural tourism and countryside management functions

In most local authorities, tourism marketing, countryside access and management work is separated, often within different departments. The projects have been able to demonstrate the advantages of these sections working together in a mutually supportive way.

Project Explore was given responsibility for the local countryside service, which greatly strengthened its impact. The Tarka Project gained credibility and practical benefits from having an otter conservation officer as part of the team. In South Somerset, a key feature of the District Council's approach to rural tourism, was a bringing together of the tourism and rights of way functions at an early stage. Rights of way were no longer seen as a highways problem, but as a tourism resource and opportunity.

This experience suggests that there are advantages in integrating tourism and countryside management. This may require simply improvement in working practices, rather than any structural changes.

Developing visitor management strategies

In many areas, there is a wealth of experience of site management techniques but less knowledge and understanding of area management.

Countryside management strategies can be valuable in identifying the needs and opportunities of a range of sites or stretches of countryside in a defined area, and in prioritising action. Often visitor management policies are contained within them, but these tend to be based on resource considerations rather than rural tourism issues. Some of the projects studied have been able to bring a better balance to this, based on practical tourism experience. The input by the North Pennines Partnership to the Area of Outstanding Natural Beauty Management Plan in that area is an example.

The Norfolk Coast Project developed its own Visitor Management Strategy based on surveys of visitors and residents, the use of four working groups to draw up different elements, and an exhaustive consultation process. This has gone on to form the basis of a very detailed visitor management action plan. Local visitor management plans for the Peak District have been referred to under traffic management.

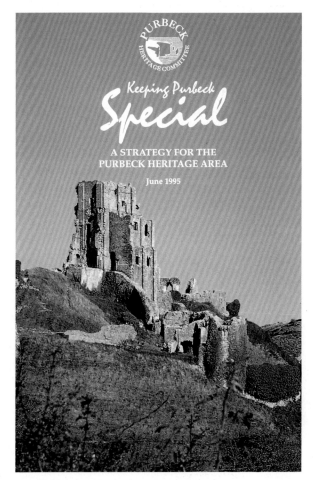

A published strategy coordinates visitor management initiatives in Purbeck.

Zoning the Norfolk coast

The Norfolk Coast Area of Outstanding Natural Beauty is a long stretch of countryside with a number of sensitive coastal wildlife sites. Parts are under considerable visitor pressure. Other areas are less visited, yet still attractive.

As a key component of the Visitor Management Strategy, an exercise was undertaken to divide the area into different zones, based on a combination of habitat sensitivity and visitor use. Six categories of zone were identified, ranging from 'areas of fragile wildlife habitat of international importance under considerable visitor pressure' to 'more robust areas, with few visitor pressures at present'. These were colour coded and displayed on a map.

Zoning reflected information from visitor surveys and site surveys across the area. One source of evidence was 'visitor incident monitoring', whereby local wardens keep systematic records for different sites, showing visitor pressure on certain days, any incidents occurring and the action taken. Ultimately, the zoning was based on the professional judgement of officers and site managers.

Visitor management policies and guidelines have been attached to the different zones, including policies towards car parking, promotion, interpretation and the development of facilities. The zoning pattern shows clearly how some areas can serve to take pressure off others.

The process provides a useful basis for commenting on planning issues, determining management priorities and allocating resources. The map is a practical, visual tool for influencing a range of organisations. It has yet to be seen to what extent it will be embraced by tourism marketing interests.

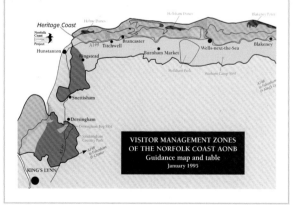

Clocktowers and cobblestones

Some 'honeypot' villages in Dartmoor National Park such as Widecombe are overwhelmed by visitors, with all the attendant problems of congestion and resentment on the part of the local community. There are other villages on the other hand, just outside the National Park, which are equally attractive but receive very few visitors and would welcome the extra trade.

Clocktowers and Cobblestones was a promotional initiative undertaken by the Dartmoor Area Tourism Initiative aimed at diverting some of this visitor pressure to some villages to the north of the Dartmoor. Twelve parishes were invited to take part in the initiative and of these seven actively supported the project. The theme of clocktowers and cobblestones was developed and some 5,000 copies of a folded, A3 sized, attractively designed, two colour leaflet were produced. The leaflet gives a description of each village and identifies points of interest, local services and walks. These were distributed in and around the Dartmoor area through Tourist Information Centres, village information points and libraries.

The parish councils were actively involved throughout and were invited to write the text describing their village and choose the illustrations. The initiative was supported by West Devon Borough Council, Torridge District Council, the Tarka Project, the parish councils and the Devon Rural Programme. West Devon Borough Council have adopted the initiative and will take it forward.

The villages involved have been enthusiastic about the initiative and feel that it will have an effect over time. Research carried out by the West Country Tourist Board suggests that the leaflet has had some, albeit limited, effect, with 14 per cent of those seeing it being influenced to visit. The economic impact of this has been equated to half a full time job equivalent. The effectiveness of the leaflet was constrained by the lack of an efficient distribution system.

Zoning is a concept which can be used in strategic visitor management, indicating areas of greater or lesser sensitivity to visitor pressure. This was a key feature of the Norfolk Coast strategy (see box on page 17). An important objective of the Dartmoor Area Tourism Initiative has been the deflection of certain forms of tourism and recreation into the fringe zone around Dartmoor rather than in the national park.

Lessons from this experience include the following:

- General countryside management plans can be strengthened by including visitor management policies informed by knowledge of tourism issues.
- Local consultation is time consuming but important if visitor management plans are to have support.
- Zoning can be a useful tool in prioritising management resources and guiding planning policies.
- To have impact, avoid confusion, and be widely used, zoning should be simple in terms of the number of zones and their meaning, but also precise in identifying boundaries.

These strategies are helpful in planning and management work; but a challenge is to find practical ways of influencing visitor behaviour based on them. A simple example is the attempt on Dartmoor to attract visitors to certain villages and away from others (see box on page 17).

Developing or improving sites

Some projects have been involved with site development projects, in order to provide appropriate additional facilities for visitors, based on new access areas or the conversion of buildings into visitor attractions. The Surrey Hills Project identified underused sites which could take more visitors and took action there. The Settle and Carlisle Company helped to win funding for visitor attraction projects at key points on the line, making use of redundant buildings. In Purbeck, proposals have been drawn up to regenerate Swanage's rundown seafront.

These schemes should lead to environmental improvement, bring economic benefit, provide additional facilities for visitors, and in some cases deflect pressure from other locations. If carried forward, they will create a tangible, lasting legacy from the projects involved.

Improving practical site management

A few projects have been involved in practical site management. The Tarka Project has undertaken otter conservation work, advised landowners and monitored possible impact of visitors on wildlife. The Dartmoor

Area Tourism Initiative selected one practical site management project to support each year. The Surrey Hills project has prepared management plans for some heavily visited sites (see box on page 19).

Two of the projects were able to work up interesting site management techniques directed at practical visitor management. In the Norfolk Coast project, a range of ways of influencing visitor behaviour and impact were tested on one fragile site, including different kinds of surfaces, barriers and wording on signs. The results were written up as a practical manual for use throughout the project area. The Surrey Hills project developed a 'Visitor Welcome Audit' as a process for checking visitor signs and facilities at all sites. Both examples demonstrate the value of a systematic approach.

Practical maintenance and improvement still demands labour and resources. © Mike Williams/CC.

Most of this work has been pursuing long term objectives, and there has been little evidence as yet of the effect on sites and visitors. Some of this is traditional countryside management work which occurs all round the country. However, these independent projects embracing sustainable tourism objectives, have been able to:

- act as a catalyst, bringing different interests together;
- be innovative and focus on particular visitor management and communication issues;
- reflect the lessons learnt back into wider tourism marketing and information functions;
- inform visitors and the local tourism industry of the importance and implications of this work; and
- provide a tangible output from the project which has helped stimulate enthusiasm and support.

Reigate Hill

Reigate Hill is a popular viewpoint on the North Downs. However, because of its location it attracts indiscriminate parking by commercial vehicles during the week and generally presents a scruffy and run-down appearance. This had long been seen as an eyesore.

In 1993, the Surrey Hills Visitor Project established a working group to look at how visitor facilities and visitor management could be improved on the site. The partners included the main landowners — the National Trust and Reigate and Banstead Borough Council — and the Countryside Commission.

This group agreed a £100,000 upgrading scheme, centred around the key car park at Wray Lane.

Proposals include moving car parking away from the viewpoint, the closure of a road, provision of a bridleway and footpath access, demolition and replacement of existing cafe and toilet block, new information centre, information boards and woodland management. These proposals are now being implemented.

The cost of the project will be largely borne by the National Trust and the Borough Council with contributions by the Countryside Commission and the Surrey Hills Visitor Project. This is the first time that the National Trust has funded a project that is not on its land. The receipts from the pay and display car park will be used over time to pay back the capital cost.

The Leland and Liberty Trails

South Somerset District Council has created regional walking routes and successfully marketed them as a significant tourism product for its area. Each route was kept quite short (around 30 miles) to meet the needs of the short break or weekend walker. They are loosely based on heritage themes, to provide an added interest and benefit from a logo for marketing and waymarking.

The walks were partly created to bring economic benefit to lesser visited parts of the District. Routes were carefully chosen to pass not only points of interest, but also villages which had accommodation and opportunities for spending.

The product is defined by a very high quality saleable pack of route cards, together with background information. The pack also contains an accommodation list and a feedback comment form.

In order not to restrict the market, no elaborate packaging has been undertaken and walkers select their accommodation from the list. However, this accommodation has been specially recruited and advised on walkers' requirements. Some walking tour operators use the routes, including English Wanderer, but most are keener on national trails and coastal routes.

Promotion has been integrated within the marketing of the District, with a sizeable feature in the destination print. Advertising in specialist media, use of an attractive flyer and distribution through retail outlets have all brought business. The routes have attracted excellent media coverage including a TV series.

The Leland Trail opened in 1990 and cost £18,000 for work on the ground, £14,000 for literature and £2,000 for advertising. A grant was obtained from the Countryside Commission. 5,000 packs were printed initially and most have now been sold, earning a small profit. Highly favourable comments have been received about the routes, and users include general tourists, groups and local people. Feedback from communities on the routes has been very positive, with a noticeable increase in spending generated.

High quality print is a key component of South Somerset's approach to promoting walking. © South Somerset District Council's Tourism & Marketing Unit.

Creating walking routes and trails

Walking is a primary activity of visitors in the countryside. It is the motivation for more than a third of day visits; and nearly one in five domestic holidays involve walking. It provides a unique opportunity for developing sustainable tourism.

Long distance walking routes have been established by three of the projects studied, in South Somerset (see box on page 19), in the North York Moors (see box on page 21) and by the Tarka Project.

The aims of those who created these long-distance routes were to:

- bring visitor spending to less visited communities (especially in South Somerset);
- deflect pressure from other over-used routes (especially in the North York Moors);
- create a resource which defines and links a new area (especially in Tarka); and
- provide a sustainable tourism product which could be marketed.

They have broadly succeeded in these aims. The routes appear well used, though not always by long distance walkers, and economic benefits have been demonstrated (eg £0.5m of visitor spending in the North York Moors). Lessons learnt include the following:

- Routes are time-consuming to negotiate and create.
- Resources must be allocated for ongoing maintenance.
- Route planning at the outset should reflect potential tourism markets. In North Yorkshire and South Somerset, the length of routes was made suitable for short breaks. In Tarka, with hindsight, the route might have been more appropriately designed to suit local use by the general holidaymaker rather than the long distance walker.
- Routes can be made more appealing and economically valuable if they link attractions and villages.
- Walking packages are not essential for generating business, but high quality information and effective marketing are needed.
- Accommodation enterprises can be encouraged to promote the routes and to meet the needs of walkers; but this is not always easy and can take time.

The vast majority of visitors who walk in the countryside are seeking short circular walks, not long distance routes. This has been confirmed in the Tarka Project, which has been increasingly working with local communities to develop circular walks. A similar community based approach has been pursued in the Wiltshire Downs. Although this kind of work is common elsewhere, for instance through the Parish Paths Partnership, the projects have been able to relate the walks to the tourism market. In South Somerset, circular walks have been actively marketed as a mainstream holiday product for many years, with good results.

Creating cycling and horse riding routes

The market for cycling and horse riding is not as large as that for walking; but it is growing more rapidly. There is an increasing interest in cycling and riding holidays. The Wiltshire Downs Project and North York Moors have developed both cycling and riding routes, and cycling routes have also featured in the Tarka Project, South Somerset, Purbeck and other projects. Lessons learnt include the following:

- Sufficient time must be allowed for careful route planning and checking.
- The market for off-road cycling trails suitable for families is particularly strong. The cycle route section of the Tarka Trail has been heavily used, with little detriment to the environment.
- To gain proper benefit from these routes, one should work closely with cycle hire and riding establishments and encourage accommodation to cater for riders and cyclists.
- Routes should provide continuous safe cycling opportunities wherever possible, not severed by main roads.

There is a growing market for cross country riding trails. © F.B. Pearce/CC.

Regional routes in the North York Moors

A joint initiative in the North York Moors National Park has created four new regional recreation routes for walkers, horse-riders and cyclists. The aim was to create some alternative sustainable routes to help ease the pressure on existing trails, and to use these routes to generate economic and social benefits for local communities.

The project has been led by the National Park but is a partnership with county and district councils, regional tourist board, Countryside Commission, Forest Enterprise and Rural Development Commission. There has also been significant involvement from accommodation and transport interests. Grants of some £30,000 were assembled from the above agencies and the national park contributed a further £15,000.

The first phase of the programme involved two routes for walkers, the Esk Valley Walk and a Link through the Tabular Hills. These opened in 1992 and 1993 and are aimed at middle distance walkers seeking a two–three day walk, the former being a walk of 35 miles from Castleton to Whitby, the latter a walk of 48 miles from Helmsley to Scarborough. The two routes were based on existing Rights of Way and were chosen to satisfy a range of criteria. These included encouraging people to stay for one or two nights in the area, the attractiveness of the routes to visitors, their accessibility by public transport, the ability to link with and encourage use of local accommodation and services, and the capacity to handle around 5,000 people a year without damage.

The routes were surveyed and extensive consultation carried out with land owners, local communities and user groups. This is time consuming but essential to build support and overcome resistance. Where necessary, improvements and upgrading were carried out and the routes were waymarked.

5,000 copies of two pocket-sized walking guides were produced, with full colour reproductions of the relevant sections of the 1:25,000 OS map and interpretation of the routes. These retail at £2.95 and are sold through tourist information centres, shops and some accommodation outlets. The walks have also been publicised through walking magazines and newspapers. A free accommodation and eating guide in the same format is available to accompany the route guides and to encourage use of local facilities.

The second phase of the project involved the creation of two further routes for horse riders and cyclists. The horse route is 35 miles long and links Pickering to Grosmont. The subject of extensive consultation with local interests and the British Horse Society, this has involved the creation of new bridleways, consideration of appropriate waymarking, parking requirements for horse boxes and location of stabling. The cycling route is some 96 miles long, laid out in a figure of eight with both on and off road sections. There are feeder routes to Whitby, Scarborough and Pickering. Both routes are due to open in 1995.

A key feature of the initiative is monitoring. Infra red detectors are used to record use of the routes; and the voluntary ranger service monitors and reports on any problems. In 1994 some 4,500 people passed along the Esk valley route and some 2,500 used the Link. Using data from previous surveys, the National Park estimate that this translates into 21,000 visitor days and spending by visitors of £0.5m, much of which will be retained locally.

Marketing sustainable tourism

Marketing, in the context of sustainable tourism, is about reaching particular kinds of visitors who may be most suited to the special needs and conditions of the local environment and economy; and projecting certain messages to them which influence how they feel about a place.

The aims of such marketing may be to:

- create awareness of an area, based on its inherent character and qualities;
- bring increased tourism spending, to assist the local economy;
- influence when people visit an area, for instance out of season;
- attract particular types of visitor who will benefit from and respect the area's environment and heritage;
- receive a higher return from visitors who do come, for example by promoting a higher proportion of staying tourism;
- promote particular products and ways of visiting which are environmentally friendly; and
- put across the possibilities for people to have a special, fulfilling experience from visiting the countryside.

Some of the projects studied have undertaken marketing activity directed outside their area; but due to limited resources they have mostly found it hard to make much of an impact. Few projects have been able to measure the results of their marketing work. Most marketing has been directed at creating awareness of these areas as destinations for walking and for low-key rural holidays, and generally projecting an image of an attractive and sensitive environment. A few projects have experimented with selling breaks or themed holidays. We look at these areas in more detail below.

Coordinating activity and pooling resources

More impact can be made if local authorities, agencies and private sector enterprises can be encouraged to work to a common marketing plan and to pool resources to implement it. This is particularly important in sustainable tourism, where agreement needs to be reached about the kind of messages to put out.

A number of projects have had considerable success in coordinating marketing activity within their areas and focusing this onto sensitive themes and images. For example, the Dartmoor Area Tourism Initiative brought together the local authorities, national park and the local tourism association to coordinate their marketing for the greater Dartmoor area, one aim being to spread visitor pressure outside the Park. The Settle and Carlisle Railway Development Company created a marketing group of all authorities along the railway line.

Establishing joint activity like this is an important way of extending the reach of the project and ensuring that sensitive marketing continues after the project has finished.

Creating a new identity for an area

Creating a new identity for an area can meet twin objectives: to help define a new tourism destination and draw attention to it, and to project a green image appropriate to the area's environment. It is particularly relevant in discrete rural areas which cut across local authority boundaries.

Using logos and themes can be an effective way to create an identity. This has been demonstrated well by the Tarka Project in promoting the concept of 'Tarka Country', with a wildlife image; and by the North Pennines Partnership, with its simple striking logo and slogan 'England's last wilderness'. Key elements of success are:

- consistent use of the theme and logo on all Project material; and
- encouraging others to use them to identify themselves with the area and for use in their marketing. In the North Pennines, many local authorities have used the logo, and a private sector publisher has come forward to create a visitor newspaper around the identity given to the area by the Partnership.

Using sensitive rural images in mainstream destination marketing. © South Somerset District Council.

Destination marketing for South Somerset

The main marketing of South Somerset as a rural destination has centred on the promotion of 'Country Breaks' through a full colour A4 sized brochure, rich with rural images. The approach has been to sell the image, but to keep the product offer quite flexible, in order to be relevant to as wide a market as possible. Therefore, the brochure contains only a few packages or specific break offers and mainly provides information on accommodation and attractions. Standardised, illustrated entries are used and prices are kept low in order to encourage maximum participation by small rural enterprises.

The brochure has been very carefully monitored. For example in 1993 this entailed:

- mailing a questionnaire to 5,000 recipients of the guide.
- producing a record pad for enterprises to use to record enquiries, and return this to the Council; and
- a printed questionnaire in the guide itself to provide feedback on visitor and activities.

From this monitoring, it was estimated that Country Breaks generated £3.5m in spending by visitors. Direct mail has been found to be a particularly effective means of promotion, and now accounts for half the distribution, based on previous enquirers and carefully targeted purchased lists.

Walking and cycling products developed by the District Council are seen as very important to this wider tourism marketing and vice versa. They are heavily featured in the brochure. A phone interview of 100 recipients found a majority reporting that the coverage of walking and cycling was critically important in encouraging them to come to the area.

Over time, the District has diminished its niche marketing of walking and cycling through specialist media as they found that this was reaching too restricted a market, with a poor cost per response. Rather, they are using these products in their more general print and campaigns, in order to attract the attention of the far wider general market for rural tourism.

Blustery breaks

Blustery Breaks was a marketing campaign by the North Pennines Tourism Partnership in order to promote the area in the off-season, based on a theme related to the environment. At the outset, the main objective was to generate media coverage to raise awareness of the area, with bookings generated from the campaign seen as a secondary benefit.

The medium used was a simple full-colour leaflet. This carried 25 entries from accommodation establishments (line drawings and text) who offered straight two–three night short breaks. The leaflet also promoted a Blustery Breaks package, involving just four accommodation enterprises and comprising a walk with a warden, talks from weather experts and visits to Widdybank Fell and Moor House weather monitoring stations. The package was run over three specific weekends in November, March and May 1993–1994; and was handled by a local company, as the Partnership did not wish to become directly involved in tour operating and wanted to support local businesses rather than compete with them.

Promotion was via the distribution of 20,000 leaflets, participation in the regional tourist boards' Borderlands campaign, and PR work.

All the package weekends ran and broke even, with 8 to 15 people on each. However, the general promotion of short breaks brought little business to the accommodation enterprises. The main success was the media coverage obtained, which was estimated to be worth around £100,000 and brought many new contacts for future use. An important additional benefit was the community spirit and enjoyment obtained from setting up and running the weekends, with tourism operators and environmentalists working together.

Bob Johnson, the Tyne Tees Weatherman, enjoys a Blustery Break. © North Pennines Tourism Partnership.

However, creating awareness of a new identity is a time consuming and potentially costly business; beware of just doing it for the sake of it.

Promoting an area as a green destination

One aspect of marketing for sustainable tourism is to try to promote an area through projecting green images in order to attract visitors who are environmentally conscious.

The Tarka Project, through the local tourist association, and the North Pennines Partnership have both undertaken separate general marketing campaigns for their areas as new green destinations. Good media coverage has been obtained; however, it can be difficult to trace this through to bookings, and there has been limited response from advertising. In South Somerset, the District Council has maintained a significant and successful destination marketing campaign, using strong rural images and green themes and products such as cycling and walking (see box on page 23). The conclusions which might be drawn from this experience are that one should:

- give priority to influencing the mainstream destination marketing activity of local authorities and tourist boards, strengthening the green images and messages they portray and the coverage given to individual rural areas (Project Explore has influenced the style and content of the South–east Cornwall main guide);
- avoid mounting small low budget advertising campaigns for separate areas;
- make full use of green themes and stories in generating press coverage, building contacts with journalists covering both travel and the environment; and
- provide back up print material to answer enquiries and stimulate interest, which can be used by others, (for example, the North Pennines has a flyer leaflet which describes the special qualities of the area and is made widely available for all local enterprises to send out).

Promoting an area as a green destination or creating a new identity for it requires sensitivity. Images should realistically portray the area for what it is. Fragile or pressurised sites should be avoided. Local people should feel happy with it and appropriate consultation is important.

Promoting short breaks, themes and packages

Marketing off-season breaks or particular activities or packages associated with the environment might appear to be a natural way of meeting many of the aims for marketing sustainable tourism. In practice this has proved difficult. A number of projects have pursued this, including Blustery Breaks in the North Pennines (see box on page 23); a short breaks campaign for

accommodation in the Settle-Carlisle corridor; and activity breaks on farms in and around Dartmoor. Another example studied is Country Village Weekend Breaks (see box on page 25). In all cases, the amount of business generated has been small, though other benefits, such as generating awareness and community participation, have been obtained.

Lessons learnt include the following:

- It is difficult to create impact from separate small budget campaigns, as concluded above.
- Unusual themed breaks can be good at generating media coverage and general awareness of an area, and are likely to lead to some business but low volumes.
- The market for people seeking tight, restricted packages is quite small.

A number of projects have concluded that 'niche' marketing based on promoting particular rural products to people with special interests is not very cost effective, in terms of numbers of visitors generated. A better approach may be to use more general marketing, projecting green images at the large number of people who are simply seeking a rural holiday and are generally interested in the environment. Imaginative ideas and opportunities, such as specific walking and cycling opportunities, or excursions by public transport, should be presented to them, but in a flexible way.

Promoting breaks in the off season can be important for businesses, and can help to secure more full time employment from tourism. There can be environmental arguments for this too, encouraging people to come when the place is less congested. However, there is little evidence that such an approach actually deflects pressures from the main season. It is also important to consider whether there are any social or environmental costs from promoting year round tourism: some local communities value the respite of a less busy period.

Building a loyal customer following

Sustainable tourism is partly about encouraging visitors to be more appreciative and understanding of the places they visit. It is about providing them with a good experience. This in turn should encourage repeat visits and recommendations. Through expanding the range of visitor experiences, all the projects have helped to bring this about. Marketing advantage could be strengthened by:

- building a database of previous visitors and enquirers and mailing to them; and
- providing a mechanism for visitors to associate themselves more closely with the area. Establishing a 'Friends scheme' and servicing members with newsletters and other material can not only provide a source of income, but also create a mailing list.

Celebrate the Countryside is a marketing campaign for the West Country based round a membership scheme and direct mailing of a newsletter (see box on page 25).

Country Village Weekend Breaks

Country Village Weekend Breaks was set up in the early 1980s as the result of a community development project in West Herefordshire.

This was a novel, imaginative idea based initially on two villages but later extended to eight villages in Herefordshire, Shropshire and Staffordshire. The emphasis was on a weekend break where visitors mixed with local people and participated in village life, breaking down the normal barriers between visitor and local resident.

Each village had a coordinator and a small committee, who put together a programme of weekends based on that village. Accommodation was provided in local farms and homes, meals provided in local pubs or cooked in local homes, and a programme of activities laid on such as guided walks, farm visits, craft demonstrations and evening entertainment. The price of a weekend break included all of the above.

A joint committee, with representatives of each of the villages, was responsible for coordinating the initiative, setting the price and marketing. In 1990, when the initiative was still going strong, about 54 different weekend breaks were available across the eight villages with a weekend costing £80. In 1989 some 350 bookings were made. Marketing was chiefly through the distribution of a small leaflet, press work and some personal contacts with travel councillors in the USA. Booking and payment was made direct to the village coordinators.

Country Village Weekend Breaks now no longer operates in England, although a sister project in Wales established in 1983 with support from the Wales Tourist Board is still in existence, as is a similar project in Northern Ireland. A number of factors contributed to its demise. The recession hit the domestic market badly and demand tailed off for what was perceived to be quite an expensive product. One village dropped out when the local pub closed and two key individuals became ill. The number of visitors was never sufficient to meet the aspirations of the villages.

Locally based and operated projects such as these are critically dependent on finding the right people with the organisational skills and time to run them. They also find it very difficult to market themselves and achieve a presence in the marketplace. The extent to which there is a market for such an organised type of package is not clear. It is interesting that in the Welsh Country Village Breaks this element has been abandoned in favour of a looser and more flexible arrangement.

Celebrate the countryside

This is a campaign launched in 1992, designed to promote the countryside of the West Country in a sensitive way. It is led by the West Country Tourist Board in partnership with the English Tourist Board, Countryside Commission, Rural Development Commission and some 16 local authorities.

The campaign aims to:
- Help build awareness of the region's countryside through exposure in the travel and countryside press;
- Create a database of countryside enthusiasts through a Green Card scheme;
- Create a vehicle for publicising small scale green initiatives and local events; and
- Establish a small environmental fund to put something back into the countryside from tourism.

The overall shape and content of the campaign is controlled by the West Country Tourist Board and a small group of the sponsoring agencies. Implementation is handled by an outside marketing agency. The budget has averaged out at around £35,000 pa, with contributions from English Tourist Board, Countryside Commission and local authorities.

Tourist Board commercial members were approached to join the scheme for a membership fee of £50. Some 50–60 members have been recruited and this income is placed into an environment fund for small scale projects. A number of small projects have been funded from the environment fund; they include nest boxes and a scheme using highland sheep to control grass in a nature reserve. These in turn have given rise to local press coverage.

A central part of the campaign has been the Green Card membership. This scheme is promoted via a leaflet (print run 100,000) which is distributed at exhibitions and through tourist information centres. It is also promoted via a coupon in the main regional guide and in press articles. Green Card Members, now numbering 3,200, pay a nominal sum (four x 25p stamps) and in return receive a quarterly newsletter giving details of environmentally friendly holidays, projects and experiences in the region. Priority is given to those local authorities participating in the scheme.

The newsletter is also sent to travel trade contacts and journalists. Familiarisation visits have been organised and this has resulted in further coverage for the scheme in national and specialist press.

A survey of Green Card members suggests that they tend to be older and more middle class than the average West Country visitor, but are regular and loyal visitors. Around half use Green Card News to plan their visits, and almost two-thirds are willing to pay for information about green tourism.

The main impact of this campaign is in providing a hook for press coverage. It has enabled the region to be featured in publications that it might not otherwise have reached; and has helped to portray a slightly different image of the West Country. It has also provided a vehicle for small scale attractions and events to publicise themselves outside the immediate locality. In addition to these benefits it is probable that Green Card News has stimulated some holiday taking in the region. The tourist board estimates that the campaign brought upwards of £1m expenditure in 1994.

Managing traffic and transport

Tourism enterprises in rural areas are heavily dependent on car-borne visitors. Yet, in many areas, concern about traffic is central to the reason for pursuing visitor management and sustainable tourism. Arguments for reducing the use of cars for tourism trips are both national, with respect to global warming, and local, with respect to congestion, local pollution and landscape degradation. For the same reasons, there is a keenness to promote public transport as an alternative.

The aims of sustainable tourism with respect to traffic and transport are to:

* manage the flow of cars and car parking so they are as unobtrusive as possible;
* reduce the proportion of visitors coming by car, in favour of other means of transport;
* support rural transport services through a greater amount of tourism income; and
* provide visitors with an alternative, enjoyable way of travelling to and in the countryside.

Across the projects studied, more time has been spent on this issue than any other. Some projects have been solely or primarily devoted to traffic and transport, while almost all the others have included it in their activities.

Areas of work have included coordinating action, traffic management strategies and plans, promoting existing public transport services and improving transport provision to meet visitors's needs and stimulate a response between participating organisations.

We discuss these approaches in more detail below.

Getting local authority departments, agencies and private transport operators to work together

One of the problems with traffic and transport management has been that different local authorities and departments are responsible for highways, car

Large numbers of cars inevitably dominate sensitive rural landscapes. © Mark Boulton/ICCE.

parking and public transport. Effective communication between them, with tourism marketing and information officers, and with transport operators is vital.

The projects have been successful in breaking barriers. In the Lake District, fora of local interests have been set up to discuss potential ways forward. In Devon and Cornwall, the Rail Partnership has brought various interests together to promote the rail network.

This experience suggests that when other areas are seeking to tackle traffic and transport issues, an independent forum or working group may be helpful.

Developing a comprehensive area strategy

Isolated schemes to promote public transport, though valuable, stand little chance of making a significant difference to the way transport is perceived in an area or to the balance of types of transport used by visitors. A more comprehensive approach may be needed.

In the Lake District, a traffic and transport strategy is being prepared to guide action across the whole national park. Components included a new road hierarchy (see box on page 29) and an integrated public transport system.

This is an ambitious strategy and it is not yet certain whether a consensus can be reached over it or whether resources can be found for its implementation. However the approach may be appropriate elsewhere, especially in other national parks and protected areas. Points to bear in mind are that it:

* avoids simply passing problems on from one site to the next;
* can enable a wide range of uses to be planned for, including non-motorised use of certain routes;
* can combine the stick of traffic management with the carrot of public transport promotion;
* is increasingly important in making a case for funding;
* forms a basis for consultation with tourism interests.

Preparing local traffic management plans for visitor pressure points

A number of projects have sought to tackle traffic and transport issues in selected beauty spots, villages or small towns which have been suffering from significant pressure. Comprehensive action programmes have been prepared, involving altering car park sizes, park and ride schemes, promoting alternative transport and signposting and visitor information. Examples include Corfe Castle in Purbeck (see box on page 27), the Hope Valley and Roches areas in the Peak District and various locations in the Lake District.

Corfe Castle

Corfe Castle is a picturesque stone village with a dramatic castle guarding a gap in the downs in Purbeck. Traffic passes through the village on its way from Wareham to Swanage and the coast. Visitors bound for the village and the coast are forced to drive through the village in order to reach the main car park. This causes traffic congestion, noise and nuisance, and detracts from the character and charm of the village.

Following extensive consultation with the local community, and other interests, a visitor management plan has been drawn up for the village which will ease some of the pressure. This has a number of components.

The National Trust, with the help of the district council has acquired the Castle View Cafe site to the north of the village. This will now become the main car and coach park for the village and castle and will also incorporate toilets and a visitor centre in the former cafe building. A footpath will link the site to the village and castle. This will siphon off some of the traffic that currently passes through the village.

The Swanage Railway has been extended from Swanage to Corfe Castle with support from the Countryside Commission. The former Corfe Castle station has been reopened and a new halt constructed at Norden to the north of the village. A park and ride facility has been developed adjacent to this by the district council with help from the Countryside Commission and the cooperation of BP who own the road access, and English China Clay, who own the site. It is hoped that this facility will divert some of the traffic between Wareham, Corfe and Swanage on to the railway.

These initiatives are being supplemented by new road signing, visitor information boards and residents parking provision in the village.

Across the roof of England

Public transport services are important to the isolated communities in the North Pennines. It was recognised that promotion of the relatively good network of existing services to visitors would strengthen them and also provide an environmentally friendly way of accessing the countryside for visitors. The North Pennines Tourism Partnership has worked with the local authorities and transport operators to produce a comprehensive public transport map showing bus and rail services across the area.

What makes this a particularly good example of its kind is the quality of the print and attention to detail, which enables the visitor to use it immediately without seeking further information. Full timetables are clearly printed on the reverse of the map. Visitor attractions are numbered on the map and text entries indicate how they can be reached by public transport. Main walking routes and cycle hire locations are shown.

Although Durham County Council is the main funder of the map, it is also supported by other local authorities and transport operators. Distribution has been via tourist information centres, accommodation establishments and the transport operators themselves, although a properly funded marketing campaign is lacking. The map is popular amongst distributors and the services appear to be doing well. A coupon in the print was returned by 140 people, 20 per cent indicating that the map was the reason for them making a trip. However, no direct monitoring of travellers to assess the true impact of the map has been undertaken.

Although these initiatives are at an early stage of implementation, this focused, integrated approach has been well received locally. Key lessons are:

- Very careful local consultation is vital, involving local residents and tourism traders. This has been a strong component in all the projects. Sometimes consensus is hard to reach. Traffic management schemes need local support to be effective.
- At the very beginning, understand the problem you are dealing with. In Borrowdale, in the Lake District, false assumptions were made about traffic flows, car parking and visitor reactions. Visitor surveys and traffic counts can help.
- Complete some early projects which people can see. This will help to maintain interest in the scheme. In the Hope Valley, swift changes were made to the Sunday rail services and promotion of the line.
- These individual projects will stand more chance of being funded and implemented if seen to be part of a wider and more comprehensive strategy. In Purbeck and the Peak District a package bid has been made to the Department of Transport for funds to implement an integrated approach.

Promoting the public transport network

In many areas, information on public transport is hopelessly fragmented and inaccessible for visitors. It needs collating and presenting in an attractive way. The majority of projects have been involved in this. A number have produced and distributed comprehensive maps of bus, rail and ferry routes, for example in the Lake District and North Pennines. Leaflets promoting individual rail lines or bus services have been produced, with information on places to visit en route. The Devon and Cornwall Rail Partnership has coordinated the production of such leaflets by working groups for each branch line and produced an overall marketing brochure and campaign for the whole network. Frequently these information leaflets refer to accessible walking opportunities, or separate publications have been produced about this. In Surrey, and in Devon and Cornwall, information boards have been erected at stations.

Feedback on the impact of such promotion has been limited, yet there are signs that it is having some effect. The Devon and Cornwall Rail Partnership recorded passenger increases of up to ten per cent per annum on some branch lines, though this project has undertaken more extensive marketing than any others, both within and outside the area. In other projects lack of resources for marketing has been a weakness. There is also some evidence from research in Devon and Cornwall that the approach is encouraging people not to use their cars, though most projects lack any detailed surveying of users which really test the impact of information on their behaviour.

Some lessons to be drawn from this experience are:

- It helps if information leaflets are directly usable. Where possible timetables should be included, as in the North Pennines leaflet (see box on page 27). In Devon and Cornwall, timetable inserts have been produced for the line guides which can be changed relatively easily.
- As much marketing back up as possible should be obtained. Tourist information centres and accommodation enterprises should be actively encouraged to display the information and it should be supported by media work and through mailing it alongside destination material.
- Consideration might be given to other ways of raising the profile of services, not just print. For example in the Lake District bus stops are being made more eye-catching using a National Park identity.

The Sunday Explorer on the Norfolk coast provides an alternative to the car. © Sarah Hunt/Norfolk Coast Project.

Improving public transport services

Often, existing public transport services are not well suited to the needs of visitors taking leisure trips in the countryside, particularly at weekends. Some projects have worked with operators to try and improve this situation. A number have succeeded in increasing the frequency of bus or rail services running on rural routes on Sundays and these services have been separately promoted, for example on the North Downs line (see box on page 30). Other initiatives have included negotiating discounts or travel pass arrangements. In the Surrey Hills, a set of new Sunday leisure bus routes has been introduced, linking countryside sites and using vintage buses and appropriately themed marketing material.

Again, while there is some evidence of demand for these Sunday services, research has not been carried out to test their impact. In the Peak District, a combination of new Sunday services, a linked shuttle bus and a new marketing leaflet coincided with a doubling of passenger levels on the Hope Valley railway line.

It appears that some important components for success with new services are that they should:

- emanate from sizeable population centres;
- link countryside sites which people really want to visit;
- have departure and return times which suit visitors' recreation needs;
- be the subject of specific marketing campaigns.

Creating a leisure experience from using public transport

Simply providing and promoting public transport services may not be enough. It is hard to persuade people to leave their cars behind out of concern for the environment. One approach is to give people a particular reason to use public transport, by identifying and promoting it as a specific leisure experience which visitors could not get in a car. Some examples of this approach which have been pursued by the projects and which could be applicable in other areas are:

- Promoting linear walks, returning by public transport: the linear fell walks leaflet in the Lake District has been popular;
- Developing and promoting cycle hire at stations, as in Barnstaple on the Tarka Line;

Cycle hire at stations gives an added reason for using the train. © Tarka Project.

- Introducing commentaries and interpretation on existing bus or rail routes;
- Promoting specific coach, bus or rail itineraries which include interpretation, for example excursions on the Settle and Carlisle Line (see box on page 30);
- Introducing guided walks from stations, for example in Devon and Cornwall; and
- Using vintage buses or steam trains can provide an extra attraction.

Many projects use striking leaflets to promote rural transport.

Lake District road hierarchy

One component of the traffic and transport strategy being prepared by the Lake District Traffic Management Initiative is a proposed new road hierarchy. This seeks to reclassify all the roads in the Lake District in a comprehensive way, and to allocate different control measures to each category.

It was felt that the current classification of roads did not reflect their ability to accommodate traffic and gave the wrong signals to motorists. All roads in the Park, including feeder roads, would be reassessed according to their type and strategic importance. A seven-layer hierarchy has been put forward, with design and traffic control standards (eg speed limits, weight limits) identified for each. A 40 mph speed limit throughout the Park has been proposed for all but Trunk roads. Many minor roads could be downgraded, with a new category of 'Lakeland Lane' which would be signed to take 'no vehicles except for access'. Special consideration will be given to the needs of walkers, cyclists and riders using roads.

The proposals were presented in a consultation document, widely distributed throughout the Lake District amongst all parties, including tourism interests. Public consultation is on-going but the proposals have proved to be controversial, with many people expressing concern about the potential impact on the area's livelihood.

The North Downs line

The North Downs line runs east-west through the Surrey Hills Area of Outstanding Natural Beauty, linking into the main rail network at Reading, Guildford, Dorking and Redhill. It is a scenic route and ideal for bringing visitors into the heart of the North Downs.

The Surrey Hills Visitor Project has progressed a number of initiatives in partnership with the County Council's passenger Transport Unit and Network South East and later, Thames Trains to increase leisure use of this line.

A two hourly Sunday service has been introduced, stopping at the rural stations which previously had no Sunday service. Tourist information points have been erected at Guildford, Shalford, Chilworth, Gomshall, Dorking, Deepdene and Reigate stations, displaying information about the local area with ideas for walks and things to see and do within easy reach of the stations. These stations have also been branded with the name 'The Surrey Hills'.

The service was originally promoted through an A2 sized colour leaflet *The North Downs line in Surrey*, providing timetable details, a line guide and suggestions for walks. Some 30,000 copies of this were produced and distributed via travel centres, libraries and information centres in Surrey and the south–west London Boroughs as well as visitor attractions served by the line. This has now been incorporated into *The Memory Lanes of Surrey* leaflet to benefit from a higher print run and more effective distribution. Other promotional initiatives included a poster with a timetable and coverage in a promotional feature in the *Sunday Express* called 'Making tracks'. This generated some 2,000 requests for further information.

The Sunday Rider ticket, a go as you please ticket, can be purchased on the trains and is valid for travel on the line. The network of Surrey leisure vintage bus services are also integrated with the train service.

Monitoring the impact of this initiative on usage has been difficult because many of the users are travelling on Sunday Rider tickets and are not counted by Thames Trains ticket receipts. The 1994 industrial action also clouds the picture and makes comparison difficult. It is proposed to carry out a survey later this year to ascertain who is using the service.

Settle and Carlisle heritage tour

This is an example of public transport marketing carried out in association with a commercial operator as a joint initiative.

The Settle and Carlisle Railway Development Company wished to generate more business for the Settle and Carlisle line, while at the same time interpreting the heritage of the line and its environment to visitors and encouraging more people to come to the area by public transport. In 1994 it established a 'Heritage Tour', as a full day itinerary by coach from various Lake District departure points. The tour visited various sites and included a one-way train trip from Settle to Kirkby Stephen. It ran every Thursday from June to October.

The Development Company negotiated a discounted fare with Regional Railways. The coach service was run by an experienced coach operator who bore the financial risk. South Lakes District Council printed a flyer leaflet for £1,000. The calculated break even point was 20 people per tour, and if this fell below 13 the tour would not run. 50 per cent of any profit (ie where loads were greater than 20) would go to the Development Company.

The tour was popular in its first year and only three were cancelled. It is set to run profitably. There has been very positive feedback from visitors. A key component has been a guided tour, by an expert, who can bring out the special features and stories for people. This year the number of tours has been increased to two per week.

The flyer leaflet is not really effective. The tour has been promoted directly through tourist information centres and other outlets in the Lake District. A high percentage of the bookings have come from the coach operator's office in Ambleside, who really gave the tour a high profile, for instance though strategically sited notice boards.

The Company is also promoting this itinerary to group organisers.

Involving the local community

Sustainable tourism must take into account the views and aspirations of the local community. This does not mean that the local community necessarily has a veto; but sustainable tourism cannot flourish in a situation where local people feel exploited, threatened or overrun by tourism.

The aims are to:

- inform local people about what is happening and maintain a dialogue with them;
- give weight to local views and involve local communities in decision making;
- raise awareness and understanding of the nature of tourism and the tourism industry and its impact on the local area;
- encourage contact between visitors and local residents; and
- protect local communities from being overwhelmed by tourism.

The projects have undertaken a range of initiatives aimed at both informing and involving local people in the planning and management of tourism in their local areas. We discuss these in more detail below.

Any rural community will have a range of opinions about tourism.
© *Peter Newton/Rural Development Commission.*

Improving communication

Informing people about what is going on and what is planned for their area is the first step in building better relationships. Most projects have produced information leaflets and regular newsletters which have been widely circulated to groups and organisations. Project Explore has used the local council newspaper, which is circulated to all households in the district, to inform people about local events. Project officers have also been active in giving presentations to local organisations. Events have been used to generate interest and publicity such as the Purbeck Aware Weekend (see box on page 33) organised by Purbeck Heritage Committee to raise interest in the project, and the Victorian festival organised by Project Explore to publicise improvements to the Looe Valley Line.

Some lessons from the projects are:

- Raising awareness with local communities takes a long time and is an almost impossible task where the project area is extensive. It is probably better to work through groups and organisations or to use specific projects as a hook.
- A flagship project, such as Project Explore's Discovery Centre can provide a visible focus for a project and help raise awareness. Some projects have found a prominently sited local office an advantage.
- The local tourism industry is often poor at putting its case across to local people. In the Peak, consultants suggested an 'open day' in the Hope Valley to improve communication between the public and local tourism operators.

Encouraging participation in decisions

Some areas have gone further than just communicating with local people and looked for ways in which to involve communities in planning and decision making.

In some areas initiatives have been undertaken directly by the local community. In the Peak, consultants were commissioned to prepare visitor management plans for two areas under the direction of local working groups with strong community representation (see box on page 32). Interpretation plans were also drawn up by local groups so that local people could select the stories and issues they wanted put across. To broaden out consultation, the Purbeck Forum was established which brings together 94 community based and other interest groups to help set the agenda and priorities for the Purbeck strategy. Consultants were used to facilitate workshop discussions.

Lessons learnt include the following:

- Local involvement and participation is a time consuming process that is often quite difficult to control and manage. Not involving people, however, can lead to serious problems when it comes to implementation of initiatives, as the Borrowdale scheme illustrated in the Lake District.
- Working through a process of discussion can help give people a broader understanding of the issues and awareness of other perspectives. It doesn't necessarily produce consensus but it can help break down hostility and improve communication.
- It is important to be clear where power lies and how much decision making has been devolved locally. It is possible to build false expectations which can lead to rapid disillusionment.
- Beware of self appointed groups or interests speaking on behalf of the community. They can be useful sounding boards but have no real legitimacy in the sense that parish or district councillors do, and may be promoting ideas which have little support in the community at large. Because of this, there is always a need to undertake wider consultation.

People often talk about local communities as though they were homogeneous which patently they are not. Local residents can be divided into many different interest groups — farmers, people who were born in the area, incomers, local shop keepers, accommodation operators etc. Some individuals will wear several hats. Within any community there will be a range of views about tourism depending on people's interests and personal circumstances. Local consultations should therefore reflect this whole range of interests.

Encouraging direct participation

Perhaps the strongest way of involving the local community in sustainable tourism is to encourage individuals or local organisations to participate directly in catering for visitors and interpreting their local area to them. This can also help to interest local residents in their own environment and to bring income to voluntary groups and community organisations.

Local events provide a particularly useful vehicle for this to happen. Only a few projects have been involved in this kind of activity. Two examples are Project Explore's 'Festival of the Sea', which included a number of community events and the Cherhill Down Ramble in Wiltshire, an arts project which involved the local community in re-chalking the white horse (see box on page 41). A particular example of a community event which includes a range of parish organisations and links tourism to a conservation theme is the Big Apple in Herefordshire (see box on page 33).

Lessons learnt include the following:

- It can be hard to get local people to take a proactive role.
- Success often depends on one or two dedicated individuals in the community who are prepared to put in a lot of voluntary effort.
- Having a motive for involvement beyond tourism, such as conservation, is important in stimulating interest.
- Working with local organisations and societies, such as Women's Institutes, can provide a useful mechanism. Tourism can be a useful source of funds for them from outside their immediate community.
- Local people can become very enthusiastic about their participation and obtain considerable personal rewards from it. Lack of visitor response can be disillusioning and so it is important that projects and events are well promoted.

Consensus building and community involvement in the Hope Valley

Local community representatives in the three parishes of Hope, Edale and Castleton were involved from the outset in drawing up a visitor management plan for the area. The process began with a community workshop, organised and facilitated on behalf of the Peak Tourism Partnership by specialist consultants. This workshop, held at Hope College on a Saturday, was held for an invited audience of over 60 local opinion leaders. It enabled the participants to identify a community agenda for tourism and to ascertain the need for producing a visitor management plan.

Following this initial meeting the three parishes and communities nominated representatives to sit on a Working Group with the various agencies and other interest groups to oversee the production of a visitor management plan. Local community representatives were also involved in selecting consultants to prepare the plan. The Working Group consisted of 32 people, including 19 who lived and worked locally, and was chaired by a local figure. The Group met with the consultants on a regular basis over the next six months, contributing ideas and influencing the final shape and content of the plan. After wider consultation at open public meetings, the plan was further modified and then adopted as a framework for future action by The Peak Tourism Partnership.

This process took a long time (over nine months) and required a lot of effort and patience on all sides. Initially the local community were both hostile and sceptical, although discussions became increasingly constructive and more consensual as time went on. The chairman of the Working Group played a key role in making these meetings work and keeping a balance between the different interests involved. This process doesn't eliminate conflict and disagreement, but it does raise awareness and change people's perceptions, and mean that the final product is more likely to be realistic and win local support.

The Working Group is keen to continue in existence in order to take an overview of the plan's implementation.

Purbeck aware weekend

This was organised over the August Bank Holiday weekend by the Purbeck Heritage Committee, to raise awareness of the special qualities of Purbeck and the need to 'Keep Purbeck Special' for future generations to enjoy.

A wide variety of activities were organised by different groups/organisations. These included farm open days, guided walks around Wareham and Swanage, and a bird watch at Durlston Country Park.

Bunches of helium filled balloons carrying the message 'Keep Purbeck Special' attracted many people to the information caravan at Studland Country Fair which contained an exhibition explaining the work of the project and its aims.

Extensive coverage was provided in local papers and on local radio and this is to be repeated as an annual event.

The Big Apple

The Big Apple is a wholly voluntary project run by the local community in seven small parishes on and below the Marcle Ridge in Herefordshire. Four weekends of events are held each year, three in the autumn, to coincide with the apple harvest, and one in May, at blossom-time. The events were started in 1989, British Food and Farming Year, and have taken place annually since then.

Orchards are a special feature of the landscape of this part of Herefordshire and the growing of dessert apples and cider fruit is important to the local agricultural economy. The Big Apple has both rural tourism and conservation objectives:

- to promote interest in English apples and cider;
- to encourage visitors and local residents to enjoy and understand the rural heritage of the area;
- to offer an opportunity for local community organisations to raise money; and
- to conserve the local orchard landscape and maintain the diversity of apple varieties grown.

Through raising interest and awareness of apples and orchards amongst local people and visitors, it seeks to promote their conservation and to encourage visitors to come to the area.

A wide range of activities are available to visitors during the weekends, all themed on apples and cider. Examples include apple displays and apple tastings, guided walks through orchards, cooking demonstrations, apple teas, farm visits and gate sales, visiting cider makers, cider tasting, folk events based on apple folklore, and practical conservation and pruning demonstrations.

The programme is run by the Big Apple Association and managed by a committee of 12 people from the various parishes. Many of the individual events are run by local groups such as the Womens Institutes, village hall committees and playgroups, who see it as a valuable way of raising funds from outside the area. School children have also been involved in various educational projects associated with the festival. Funding is largely self-generated, with occasional small grants for specific events from the Countryside Commission.

Annual visitor numbers in total over the four weekends are around 1,500 to 2,000. The majority of visitors are local or from the West Midlands region, with around 20 per cent staying away from home. Promotion is through a simple leaflet, free media coverage and direct mail. The latter has proved particularly important, with a high proportion of repeat visitors. The Big Apple has helped to create an image for the area and apples and cider are now being used more heavily in the promotion of Herefordshire as a whole.

The Big Apple shows how community participation and local distinctiveness can be promoted as a tourism asset while also seeking conservation objectives. There is considerable enthusiasm amongst the local community in welcoming visitors, although much of the organisation rests on the voluntary efforts of a few key individuals.

Apple displays and apple tasting bring visitors into contact with local people. © Richard Denman.

Increasing local benefit

One of the main tenets of sustainable tourism is that tourism should benefit the locality in which it takes place. In other words sustainable tourism is more than just about reducing the negative effects, it should actually make a positive contribution to the local environment and local well being.

The aims are to:

- stimulate more visitor spending in the local area;
- encourage the tourism industry itself to source more of its supplies locally;
- ensure that local enterprises are equipped to benefit from tourism;
- encourage visitors to contribute to conservation and the cost of visitor management in a destination.

The projects have experimented with a range of initiatives designed to achieve the above objectives. Local producer groups have been established to encourage visitors and other enterprises to purchase local products. A number of schemes have been set up to try and raise additional money for conservation projects from visitors by encouraging voluntary donations. A few projects have provided training and business advice to raise the professionalism of local businesses and enable them to capitalise on tourism. We discuss these approaches in more detail below.

Establishing local producer groups

Promoting local products such as crafts, food and drink to visitors is relevant to sustainable tourism in that:

- it can provide a useful source of revenue for small scale local enterprises often sited in isolated communities and which have limited resources and skills in marketing;
- it provides visitors with a particular flavour of the local area, and can be used in promoting this distinctiveness to them;
- these are products which local tourism enterprises themselves can use, so enhancing their own local character and putting more money back into the local economy.

Several projects have established groupings of local producers with the aim of encouraging networking and raising their profile with visitors. Activities have included the production and distribution of a leaflet, usually in the form of a trail, attendance at craft and country shows and press work.

Two successful groups have been established in the Yorkshire Dales (see box on page 35). In the Tarka Project some 20 enterprises producing crafts and foods have got together to promote their products to visitors as well as to other tourism enterprises. The Dartmoor Area Tourism Initiative have formed the Dartmoor

Sampling local produce can be a special experience for visitors.
© *Richard Denman.*

Area Producers group and produced a report featuring some 50 producers, although keeping this group going has proved difficult. In the North Pennines a formal group has not been established although producers are featured in a North Pennines Produce Trail, and training workshops are being run for producers.

Lessons learnt include the following:

- These groups can form a useful function and can indeed generate additional business. Half the North Pennines producers have reported additional business coming from the trail. Visitor awareness of the Yorkshire groups is high.
- The value can come as much from exposing local products to other enterprises as from promotion to visitors. The Tarka group has been deliberately established as part of the local tourist association to assist this process.
- Groups require a lot of 'hand-holding' and support to get established, are often quite fragile and their success is critically dependent on the enthusiasm and commitment of the people involved. Without a few key committed individuals these groups can easily falter. Enterprises that are more businesslike in their attitude are more likely to make a go of this. Groups work best when they are kept to a modest size.

Raising money from visitors

A number of projects have experimented with schemes to encourage visitors to make a voluntary donation towards environmental and conservation projects which benefit the area. Various research amongst visitors has consistently shown that visitors themselves are willing to contribute. This was reaffirmed by research carried out by the Peak Tourism Partnership. The problem has been to find the right mechanism to tap this source of funding.

In the Peak District a voluntary donation scheme has been set up in accommodation establishments and in car parks (see box on page 37) and funds raised will be channelled into conservation projects through a special trust which has been established for this purpose.

Yorkshire Dales food and craft workshop trails

Two successful producer groups have been set up in the Yorkshire Dales, one focused on craft workshops and the other on food and drink producers. Both groups produce and distribute a leaflet and cooperate on other areas of joint marketing. The Rural Development Commission has been instrumental in establishing these groups with the aim of stimulating business activity and growth in the rural economy. The tourist board and national park were in favour of these initiatives because they were providing wet weather attractions and alternative places to visit to the more congested areas of the Dales.

The Dales Country Workshop Trail was established in 1990. The Rural Development Commission invited appropriate businesses to an evening meeting to float the idea and subsequently chaired meetings for the first year and provided some administrative support until the group was sufficiently organised to take over. Businesses had to meet certain criteria such as generating employment, in business for at least a year, being capable of receiving visitors without planning or highway problems, able and willing to demonstrate crafts to the public. Some pump priming grant aid was provided by the Rural Development Commission, the local authorities and the Yorkshire and Humberside Tourist Board.

The Workshop Trail now has 13 members in an informal grouping, including potters, furniture makers, a sculptor and a jeweller. They meet several times a year and charge a flat membership fee of £350 to cover the cost of joint marketing activity. The main promotional tool consists of a two colour, attractively designed leaflet (one-third A4 size). Some 120,000 copies are produced each year and distributed by a brochure distribution company to tourist information centres, attractions and accommodation establishments within the surrounding area. They also make use of leaflet swaps organised by the tourist board, and a poster (500 copies) has been produced to use in conjunction with the leaflet. The main concern of the group is to try and boost visitors in the shoulder periods.

The Yorkshire Dales Fine Food and Drink Trail was established somewhat later in 1994, but has followed a similar pattern and covers a similar geographical area. As with the workshop trail the Rural Development Commission helped to establish the group and a small amount of pump priming funding from the Rural Development Commission and local authorities helped fund the initial leaflet and get the initiative up and running. There are six members altogether including a brewery, trout farm and Wensleydale Creamery and they meet every two months.

A press launch helped provide some useful initial publicity and, like the workshop trail, they produce and distribute around 100,000 copies each year of a small, but professionally produced leaflet. In addition they have instigated a passport system — visit all six attractions and get a free T-shirt; and are planning to sell each others products in their shops. A Food and Drink Trail Fortnight is to be staged at the Wensleydale Creamery in 1995. The group is also thinking about having a video made to send to stimulate interest amongst travel and food journalists in press and TV.

These trails are seen as complementary to other marketing activity carried out by the individual members, rather than replacing the need for individual marketing. Research carried out by students from a local college for the workshop trail in 1993 showed that 30 per cent of visitors to the Dales had heard of the workshop trail and that half of those had found out about it from the leaflet. Two-thirds of respondents agreed that visiting one workshop, prompted them to visit another and a majority said that they would visit more than one whilst in the area.

The six businesses in the food and drink trail already attract 400,000 visits between them and the trail represents a relatively small part of their total marketing spend. Nevertheless they see it as a sensible and cost effective addition to what they are already doing. Research on visitors to the trail is planned for this year.

Key factors in the success of these examples appear to be keeping the group small and intimate, developing the right chemistry amongst the participants, the businesslike attitude of the enterprises and the initial support, encouragement and expertise to get the initiative off the ground.

Cheese making in Wensleydale, supported by visitor income. © *Rural Development Commission.*

Specially adapted ticket machines encourage visitor donations in the Peak Park. © Peter Ashcroft/CC.

A similar mechanism has been used on Humberside to raise funds for nature conservation through the Birds of the Humber Trust (see box on page 38). Projects are also being established in South Devon drawing on hotels that are already participating in the green audit initiative and in the North Pennines where an existing trust will be used to disperse the funds. In South Devon, a different approach involved the selling of a book of discount vouchers with the proceeds going to environmental projects (see box on page 37). Tarka has established a Friends of Tarka scheme which invites visitors to make a donation to support local conservation, although take up has been limited to date.

This approach is still in its infancy and it is too early to judge whether it will take off. So far the amounts raised have been limited in relation to the effort expended.

Lessons learnt include the following:

- Potentially large sums could be raised by accommodation operators or other enterprises adding a small levy to bills, which customers can opt not to pay. Where this has been tried, visitors have been very supportive. However, some projects have found enterprises to be wary of getting involved in a levy scheme. An alternative has been simply to place donation boxes in establishments, although there is little evidence as yet about how much money this might raise.
- Donation opportunities in car parks offer a promising way of raising funding and also a way of reaching the day visitor.
- Voucher schemes also appear to be worth looking into, as they give the visitor some tangible benefit as well as raising money.

- Establishing separate trusts is a time consuming and expensive business and this can only really be justified if the funds raised are likely to be significant. In most instances using established conservation organisations or existing trusts will make more sense.

Enabling local enterprises to capitalise on tourism

Success in increasing local benefit from tourism is partly dependent on the many scattered and small enterprises which make up the rural tourism product being helped to run profitable businesses, market themselves effectively and provide the visitor with a good experience. It also depends on people living in local communities who have land or resources, such as farmers, being given the right guidance on tourism development opportunities.

Some of the projects have helped in this process through marketing schemes or strengthening local tourist associations, which are referred to in other sections. A few have been more directly involved in helping local businesses through training. The Wiltshire Downs Project set up some marketing and management training courses for small businesses but levels of participation were low. The Dartmoor Area Tourism Initiative funded three pilot projects on farms to develop small scale farm tourism initiatives and disseminated the results of these to other farmers through seminars. This appears to have been successful in developing interest. By far the greatest involvement in training, however, has been in the North Pennines where a separate Business and Training Initiative was established with independent funding to run in parallel with the Tourism Partnership, which has handled over 700 business enquiries and 175 in depth advisory sessions and has organised or helped promote 82 training events in the area.

The experience from the projects suggests that, to make an impact, training needs to be:

- delivered as locally as possible within communities, as this increases take up;
- preferably worked up over time with the participation of local enterprises themselves and delivered through a well resourced and coordinated project; and
- focused on a specific topic which is already known to be of interest to enterprises, especially if a one off course or workshop.

The whole area of training for rural tourism enterprises, and of farm diversification into tourism, is a large one. Many organisations are involved such as the Regional Tourist Boards, Rural Development Commission, Training and Enterprise Councils and ADAS. Many areas have active local enterprise networks, such as farm holiday groups. In general it makes sense for work in this area not to be separated out under a label of sustainable rural tourism but integrated within existing programmes. However, there may be merit in establishing well focused, and locally based joint initiatives, between these agencies in some carefully selected areas.

Peak District tourism and environment fund

The Peak Tourism Partnership has established a mechanism to raise funds from visitors and channel these into visitor management and conservation projects in the Peak District. This is based on an idea first proposed in a report commissioned by the English Tourist Board and Countryside Commission in 1992.

In 1993 research was undertaken by the Partnership, using a research student from Sheffield Hallam University, to examine visitors' attitudes to donating to environmental projects. In this survey, 75 per cent of visitors agreed with the principle of visitors contributing directly to local conservation and environmental works. There was also support for this to be collected through voluntary levies and distributed to projects via a central pool.

In the light of this survey the Partnership worked up a scheme in association with a consultant paid for by the Countryside Commission. It was decided to initiate two pilot fund raising schemes based on accommodation outlets and car parks. Some 40 accommodation outlets from all over the Peak District elected to take part in the scheme. Guests are invited to make a voluntary contribution and collecting boxes, leaflets and posters have been provided by the Partnership. Operators were unwilling to impose a voluntary levy on hotel bills, although this has been tried effectively elsewhere.

The car park scheme has been initiated in the High Peak Borough Council car parks in Castleton, Hope and Edale.

Visitors are asked to make a voluntary contribution by means of an explanatory notice board next to a dedicated ticket machine in the car park. The local authority were unwilling to collect the donations through overpayment in their own pay and display machines.

A Trust has been established to administer the funds collected from the above initiatives and to channel these into suitable projects across the Peak District. Conservation organisations and other groups will be asked to bid for funds on an annual basis. The costs of establishing the Trust and the two pilot schemes were met from the Countryside Commission, Rural Development Commission, East Midlands Electricity, Center Parcs and the Metric Group. The Trust will continue in existence after the Partnership has been wound up.

The pilot schemes were launched in August 1994. It is early days to gauge the success of this project as it has yet to be in place over a whole season and resource input has been relatively limited. The car parks scheme has proved to be the most effective, collecting £800 in the first six months. The car parks frequented by walkers provide the bulk of this. The accommodation outlet collection scheme did not commence operation fully until Easter 1995. The Partnership has now extended the coverage of the existing schemes to include over 100 accommodation and retail outlets and a further two car park collection points.

Two schemes have already been grant aided: one is the production of a teachers' information pack, and the other advisory road signs.

Raising funds through discount offers — Cockington Country Park

This scheme was run by the South Devon Green Tourism Initiative, to test a method of raising money from visitors to put towards conservation activity. It is particularly interesting as it provides clear marketing advantages for the businesses contributing and also saves money for visitors, so the environment, the industry and the tourist all benefit.

Cockington Country Park is in a secluded valley in Torbay Borough and receives 300,000 to 400,000 visitors per year. There are various traders in the park, selling a range of foods and crafts. They conceived of the idea of discount vouchers to attract more business. This struck a chord with the Devon Wildlife Trust who had been thinking about such a scheme as a way of raising funds for conservation.

Initially, a booklet of vouchers from nine traders, providing discounts to the value of around £2.50 (money off from specific purchases etc) was produced

and sold for £1 at the Park centre. Over a few summer months it only raised £45. Feedback from visitors suggested that they would have been very happy to donate to an environment fund if asked directly, but the vouchers were irrelevant to them as most had already visited the Park when they came across the booklet, or felt they would not be staying long enough to use it.

Rather than give up, the scheme was redesigned to take account of this feedback. The discount vouchers were printed as part of a colour brochure to Cockington, 60,000 of which were distributed throughout Torbay. They therefore had much more promotional value and visitors could plan their trip around using them. They were validated by a stamp on arrival, for which the visitor paid £1. This validation money raised £2,456 between Easter and September 1994.

Birds of the Humber Trust

The Humber Estuary and coast of Humberside have some of the best bird watching sites in Britain. This initiative is designed to generate funds from visitors to the area and channel the money raised into visitor management and interpretation at bird watching sites along the Humber Estuary.

The idea was originated by a consultant who was putting together a bird watching guide and some associated marketing proposals for Humberside County Council. The County was looking for ways to diversify and develop tourism interest in the area. Birds of the Humber Trust was developed as a parallel initiative to this and seen as a way of putting something back into nature conservation and demonstrating that tourism and conservation could be mutually supporting.

An independent trust was established as the best mechanism to oversee the initiative, attract funding and channeling money to suitable conservation projects. Humberside County Council approached BP, who have a factory on Humberside, who agreed to sponsor the project and provided £30,000 towards the set up costs. Humberside County Council provided officer and administrative support. Trustees included representatives of the sponsors, Hull University, councillors and the MP. They meet three times a year.

Income for the Trust is generated through grants, donations and fundraising activities. Grants to date have comprised £5,000 from BP and £10,000 from Humberside County Council on an annual basis. Other income earning activities have included a project with local accommodation, sales of souvenirs and guides, attendance at public shows and exhibitions and various fund raising events. These activities are detailed below:

- Some 60 accommodation operators on Humberside were approached to take part in a voluntary levy scheme and 25 agreed to participate, although none were prepared to add a levy to guest bills. Most operators are simply leaving a collecting box in reception although some actively promote the scheme to customers. In the first 12 months the accommodation scheme has generated £50.
- Sales of merchandise, eg T shirts, key rings, notepads etc, at events and shows have raised some £250.
- A sponsored 24 hour birdwatching bicycle race raised £500 and £300 has been raised from donations from people participating on bird walks as part of the guided walk programme organised by Humberside County Council.

Income is redistributed to conservation projects through nominated conservation bodies such as the county wildlife trust. Grant applications are sought on an annual basis. To date some four grants worth £9,800 have been distributed. Projects include part funding of a Little Tern warden at Spurn Heritage Coast, part funding of a management plan for Spurn Peninsula, interactive displays in Cleethorpes Discovery Centre and a grant towards a local RSPB members group. Some five projects have been put forward for funding in 1995–1996 totalling some £8,500.

The project has provided some funding for local conservation projects and helped raise awareness of the conservation issues in the area. An independent body is much better placed than a local authority to raise money from sponsorship and voluntary contributions although establishing a trust requires a lot of time and effort. Effective fund raising requires an ongoing commitment of time, enthusiasm and expertise. One of the lessons from this project is that without a continuing staff input progress will be limited.

Changing visitor attitudes and behaviour

A high priority should be given to influencing visitors who are already in the area. These people are relatively easy to reach, and many will be frequent visitors. Influencing their behaviour, raising their awareness of the issues, increasing their understanding and enlisting their help, is a valuable tool for sustainable tourism. Raising environmental consciousness in one area may influence people's attitudes when visiting other destinations.

The aims include:

- increasing visitors' understanding of the sensitive nature of the area, its heritage, wildlife, community etc;
- encouraging visitors to go to specific places or take specific routes;
- changing the behaviour of individuals and groups of countryside users;
- promoting longer stays and encouraging the purchase of local goods and services; and
- increasing enjoyment and enriching the visitor's experience.

Trying to influence existing visitors has been central to all of the project studied.

A variety of tools and techniques have been used to pursue the above aims with a mixture of results, including provision of leaflets, establishing visitor centres, holding events and extending interpretation. We discuss these in more detail below.

Producing information print

The projects have produced a large number of information leaflets between them which seek to influence where visitors go and what they do and provide some environmental interpretation. Broadly these fall into the following categories:

- General information and orientation leaflets covering the whole area based on a map. These have been produced for the North Pennines, Wiltshire Downs, and the Dartmoor area, amongst others. This kind of print is potentially very valuable as a tool in visitor management as it can influence visitor movement, refer to the sensitivity of certain sites, and promote different forms of access. It also helps to create an identity for an area.
- Visitor newspapers and guidebooks. A separate 'green guide' has been produced for Tarka Country and visitor newspapers in North Norfolk and the North Pennines. The latter give good scope to put over conservation messages and information about conservation activity alongside practical visitor information. It is also possible to have these produced commercially while still ensuring they reflect sustainable tourism objectives, as in the North Pennines.

- Individual leaflets on themes or sites, such as leaflets on walking and cycling or on cultural or environmental themes. Almost all projects have produced these. They have a varying impact according to their quality, print run and method of distribution.

There is a great temptation to produce leaflets as they provide something tangible to show and are popular with local communities and the people who devise them. They can be a cost effective way of reaching an audience but the influence on visitors of print produced by the projects is hard to assess and there has been little monitoring of it. Their experience suggests that:

- Distribution is critical if print is to have any value and so outlets should be identified and resources set aside for this from the beginning.
- Impact and usability will determine effectiveness. Information print should give visitors enough detail so that they can act upon it without recourse to further information.
- Wherever possible it is worth trying to measure the impact of print. This is best done through visitor surveys, but even a small feedback coupon for people to send back will give a comparative measure of its usefulness.
- It is better to improve the distribution of existing print than produce other titles which might duplicate what is already available.

Effective distribution and working with outlets

The importance of effective distribution identified above has been recognised by many projects. Some have used commercial distribution mechanisms or established their own. The Tarka Project and the Dartmoor Area Tourism Initiative produced their own distinctive literature display racks. Some projects have identified information outlets within rural communities, such as in pubs and shops.

The importance of having information in accommodation enterprises is increasingly recognised. This is a key theme of the Tarka Country Tourism

Using local materials to provide a literature rack with a difference.

Association, who distribute to their members. The South Devon Green Tourism Initiative has placed emphasis on encouraging accommodation establishments to carry information for visitors, for example on notice boards or special green files in bedrooms.

Projects have found that a lot has depended on the enthusiasm of individuals and whether they actively try to interest enquirers in environmental issues. Training events for information staff or accommodation operators can help here. A good example was the 'Countryside Awareness Day' in South Devon where tourism operators met conservationists to learn about local sites and issues.

An important principle is to try to intercept visitors where they are, rather than relying on them to go and seek information.

Developing strategic visitor centres

A number of projects have considered the role of visitor centres in managing visitors. These usually include an information desk, shop, exhibition area and toilets; they may incorporate a networked tourist information centre. There are two conflicting schools of thought here. The first is that visitor centres can act as a gateway to an area, intercepting visitors, introducing them to what the wider area has to offer and helping to disperse them to less visited sites. This is how Project Explore sees the Discovery Centre it created in Looe (see box on page 41) and the role that Purbeck see for four proposed visitor centres in Purbeck. The alternative view is that visitor centres attract and concentrate visitors and make the problem worse. This was a concern expressed by the local community in Castleton in the Peak District.

Visitor centres are costly to build and more importantly represent a continuing burden on resources in terms of their management and upkeep, although interestingly the Discovery Centre in Looe is staffed by volunteers.

The experience of the projects suggests that:
- Visitor centres can help to raise awareness and interest in the surrounding area but that they need to be located where the visitors are. It is not clear that visitor centres act as an attraction in their own right.
- Visitor centres don't have to be stand alone. The Tarka Project helped to establish a very small centre within a commercial garden centre. More imaginative use might be made of existing venues to display information about the wider area.
- Community involvement in centres and the incorporation of community facilities needs to be considered. This has become an important issue with a proposed centre in Alston in the North Pennines.

Traditional events appeal to visitors, but information is needed about them. © Mark Boulton.

Organising and promoting events

Guided walks, talks, wildlife discoveries, country shows and many other kinds of event can be highly effective in giving visitors a true feel for the area they are visiting and conservation issues at first hand. A number of projects have compiled their own programme of events, bringing together all those laid on by different organisations and voluntary bodies in their areas. The Dartmoor Area Tourism Initiative project ran an events hotline as a telephone enquiry service, though response was limited. A few projects, such as Project Explore, have organised their own events. The experience suggests that:
- Both compiling event information and running events is very time consuming, which has caused some projects to stop doing this.
- There is a feeling that events are only reaching the converted, and often the same local people. To try to overcome this, Project Explore took an event to where tourist were, via a beach puppet show, and also put on and promoted a special collection of events as a 'Festival of the Sea'. More of this kind of approach might be tried.
- There may be a case for wider marketing of events, in print aimed at visitors, such as in the comprehensive Green Guide to Cornwall which features Project Explore events alongside others.
- Events can provide an excellent opportunity for creativity and involving the local community. The Cherhill Down Ramble, part of the Wiltshire Downs Project, is a good example (see box on page 41).

The South–east Cornwall Discovery Centre

The Discovery Centre comes under the umbrella of Project Explore. As a visitor centre, its aim is to introduce visitors to the culture, heritage and countryside of the surrounding area, inspire them to explore it in a sensitive and appropriate way and to encourage them to come back outside the peak period.

Based in an attractive purpose built building it is located in the main car park in West Looe, a popular holiday and day visit destination in South-east Cornwall. There is no admission charge and it is staffed by volunteers drawn from a pool of fifty local people, coordinated by a part-time manager employed by the District Council. Inside it consists of a shop and information centre on the ground floor with an exhibition area above. The exhibition area is flexible and can be used as a meeting room or for audio-visual presentations. Public toilets adjoin the building.

Total floor area of the building is 170m² and the cost of construction and fitting out was £194,000.

The cost was met by Caradon District Council with just over half being funded by grants from the Rural Development Commission, Countryside Commission and the European Union. The centre opened in 1992 and attracted 114,000 visitors in its first year of operation. Its location is recognised to be crucial to its success, as it is prominently sited in the main visitor car park and intercepts visitors on their way to and from the town.

The Discovery Centre appears to be fulfilling its aims. A survey carried out in 1992 found that 85 per cent of the people using the centre were holidaymakers staying in and around the area. Three-quarters of these were just passing, rather than seeking the centre out, and 50 per cent said they had learned something new about South–east Cornwall. Just under a third of visitors asked for some specific advice or information and the majority intended to take some action as a result. 44 per cent of visitors noticed the events being offered and ten per cent said they intended to participate.

The Cherhill Down Ramble

The Cherhill Down Ramble was a community arts and access event initiated by the Wiltshire Downs Project. It was enacted over four consecutive evenings, July 7–10, 1994.

The objectives were to involve the local community in their environment and its conservation, to make them more aware of its heritage and recreation opportunities, to raise awareness of the Wiltshire Downs area, and to provide an event for visitors.

The event centred on the re-chalking of the Cherhill White Horse. It was a true partnership event between organisations. The Parish Council owned the White Horse and were looking for ways to restore it given limited funds and local interest. National Trust owned the land around the Horse and provided the materials, as they also wanted to see the Horse restored and to publicise access to the Downs. The re-chalking was carried out by the British Trust for Conservation Volunteers working with local people and the National Trust.

To celebrate the re-chalking, a special play was devised by Theatre in the Downs, a local professional company. They involved the local schools and many village community groups, who re-enacted scenes from the village's history including the construction of the Horse. The play involved a 2.5 mile ramble from the village to the Horse and hillfort, with various happenings on the way.

Tickets were restricted to 200 per event and were completely sold out, raising over £3,000. Grants were obtained from Rural Action, the Foundation for Sport and the Arts, and the District Council. The total cost of the event was £12,000 including production costs and fees.

Good publicity was obtained for the area, including radio and TV coverage. Displays were mounted in local shops and tourist information centres. The community now have a new pride in their environment, and have the skills to work with the National Trust on maintaining the Horse.

An excellent, creatively designed report on the event has been produced as guidance for others, and is available from Kennet District Council.

A 'white horse', carried by six local boys, leading the ramble.
© Paul Greenway/Wiltshire Downs Project.

Interpretation strategies and techniques

A systematic approach to interpretation of the environment to visitors has been important in some projects. A key aspect has been to involve others in this. This can occur at different levels. For example, in the Peak District a bottom-up approach has been adopted, with a series of local interpretation groups working at a community level to decide what aspects of the local area they wish to bring out and how to do it, aided by external consultants as facilitators. In the Tarka Project, the various environment and heritage agencies in the area have been brought together to agree a common interpretation strategy. Both approaches are valuable in ensuring that the interpretation activity lives beyond the end of the project.

Two important areas of interpretation with which the projects have been involved, and which present environmental issues in a creative way are:

- Working with children and education groups. The Devon and Cornwall Rail Partnership introduced an activity pack for the Tarka Line, with games and quizzes. The Settle and Carlisle Company worked with teachers to prepare and distribute a detailed education pack to attract school groups to the line. Other projects have worked with local schools or held family events. This kind of work can have an influence on possible visitors of the future.
- Using the arts in interpretation. This has been very well demonstrated by the Wiltshire Downs Project, which is part funded by Southern Arts. Activities have included theatrical events, such as the Cherhill Down Ramble, using a local artist's work in print, and preparing an attractive guide to local arts and crafts. Other projects could benefit from a closer partnership between arts and countryside work, and put across messages in a more subtle and less heavy handed way than more traditional interpretation. This can strengthen the visitor appeal of sites and events.

Greening the visitor

Encouraging visitors to be environmentally responsible can be approached through putting over more direct messages to them. Two ways in which projects have been involved in this are:

- Green codes or tips for individual visitors. The Dartmoor Area Tourism Initiative Project prepared a *Green Visitor Guide*, with ideas on how to behave in an environmentally friendly way, illustrated with cartoons. It was not easy to distribute and effects were not monitored. In South Devon, hotels have been advised about giving direct and specific messages to guests, for instance on reducing demand for the washing of towels (see box on page 46). The

Norfolk Coast Project has promoted its green visitor code heavily, and has occasionally paid for it to be inserted in holiday guides.

- Influencing specific types of visitor. Group visits can be potentially more damaging to the environment than individual trips. However, there is a mechanism for getting through to groups via operators. In the Peak District, work with activity centres on codes of conduct has been proposed. In Dartmoor, the Dartmoor Area Tourism Initiative produced a guide for coach operators to dissuade them from using certain routes or sites and recommending alternatives (see box on this page). Some conclusions from this experience are that:
- It is hard to get general codes across to individual visitors. They are hard to monitor and their value is not yet proven.
- Specific messages at the point of action may well work but they need to be very carefully worded so that the visitor understands the reason and is not confused about the action to be taken.
- Influencing group visits through liaison with operators or user groups can be effective.

Coach drivers' handbook

Building on work carried out by the Dartmoor National Park, the Dartmoor Area Tourism Initiative produced a publication aimed at coach operators and drivers. The aim was to encourage coaches to use the most suitable routes and also to include areas outside the National Park in their tours. The handbook sets out five suggested routes with some interpretation, lists visitor attractions, refreshment stops, coach parking facilities and provides some background information about the area and its sensitivity.

The handbook was produced in consultation with the National Park, Devon County Council Transport Coordination Centre, the Bus and Coach Council and the Coach Drivers' Club. Some 2,000 copies of the A4 sized, 13 page guide were distributed to coach operators that already visited the area using existing mailing lists and observation. The emphasis was on existing users, not on encouraging more coaches.

A questionnaire sent out to those who had received the handbook produced a favourable response and a local company adopted two of the suggested routes outside the National Park for its programme. Hatherleigh and the Tamar Valley attracted more coaches as a result. This publication has now been adopted by the National Park.

Influencing tourism enterprises

Tourism enterprises have a central role to play in fostering sustainable tourism. The way they conduct their business forms an important component of the impact of tourism on the environment. They are also very well placed to influence the behaviour of their guests, and may in turn benefit from the growing market of visitors who are concerned about the environment. The use of environmentally friendly materials by tourism enterprises can benefit local suppliers.

The aims are to:
- encourage enterprises to understand and adopt the general principles of sustainable tourism;
- reduce the impact of tourism enterprises on the local and global environment, through use of energy, waste treatment etc;
- assist enterprises to benefit from operating in an environmentally friendly way; and
- encourage enterprises to put over relevant information to their visitors.

Most tourism projects have worked on building a close relationship with tourism enterprises in their area and have encouraged them to support sustainable tourism principles and the work of the project. A number have also tried to influence their environmental practices. We discuss these initiatives in more detail below.

Encouraging involvement

Some of the projects have had private sector representation on their steering groups, but this mainly served to influence the projects themselves rather than work the other way. Primarily, bridges with the local tourism industry at large had to be built during the course of the projects.

Some of the techniques employed included:
- Mailing to enterprises — although one off mailshots often have little effect, as was found in the South Devon Initiative.
- A sustained campaign of communication, including mailing regular newsletters, holding meetings, and maintaining a central office which people could drop into at any time. Many projects used this approach, and it has largely paid off. It was particularly successful in the North Pennines, where an independent survey found awareness of the project to be very high.

- Work with existing tourism associations or similar trade groups. This has tended to work well. The Dartmoor Area Tourism Initiative helped the Dartmoor Tourist Association double its membership during the course of the project. The South Devon Initiative found it to be essential as a way of getting green messages across to a large number of enterprises cost effectively.
- Helping to form a new association. This has been successfully achieved in the Tarka Project (see box on page 44) and the North Pennines and is being pursued in the Wiltshire Downs.
- Holding regular forums for enterprises round the area. South Somerset District Council concluded that their area was too large for a tourism association to operate effectively. Regular local feedback meetings have worked well for them.

Some conclusions which can be drawn from the experience of the projects are that:
- A key to success has been to adopt a personal approach rather than trying to influence enterprises from a distance.
- Understandably, enterprises are primarily concerned about short term issues and profitability. This makes it less easy to interest them in environmental issues. Although, by and large, they have been receptive over time.
- Influencing just a few key individuals and then using them to influence their peers has proved to be a successful approach, especially in the South Devon Initiative.
- Networks such as tourist associations are critically important in influencing tourism enterprises. However, tourist associations are by their nature fragile organisations, usually with few resources, which rely on the work of enthusiastic individuals. They tend to need constant support and encouragement if they are to be effective. They can provide a valuable mechanism for maintaining interest in sustainable tourism after the end of the project, but they may not be able to sustain this over time without the support of local authorities or other agencies.

All in all, most projects have worked hard at liaison with tourism enterprises and have had some success. The development of two significant new networks in Tarka Country and the North Pennines, which have adopted green principles and are themselves trying to put them into effect, is a particular achievement.

The Tarka Country Tourist Association

The Tarka Country Tourist Association was launched by the Tarka Project after three years, as a mechanism for getting the private sector operators involved, supporting and benefiting from the project. Up until then, there had been relatively little response from individual enterprises.

It was set up by selecting specific enterprises, which were approached independently by the project officer. The concept was put to them of forming a group who would work together on information and marketing initiatives. A working group and committee structure was established. From these beginnings, membership has snowballed and now stands at 150, with a target of 240 in three years time.

The Association has a number of features which make it relevant to sustainable tourism and different from most local tourist associations:

- The type of enterprise involved is varied. As well as accommodation and attractions, it includes pubs, shops, transport operators etc. A separate 'Producers Group' of craft and food producers has been formed within the Association. In this way, the members can benefit each other, use each other's services and promote them to their visitors.
- The Association was founded on green principles. To qualify, members have to sign a Green Charter, which commits them to:
  - Environmentally sound practices — products used, recycling, energy and waste.
  - Promoting walking, cycling, horse riding and public transport to visitors.
  - Providing visitors with information on wildlife and encouraging them to respect the life and work of the countryside.
  - Managing their ground and buildings in an environmentally friendly way.
  - Actively supporting conservation in the area.
  - Favouring local products where possible.
- A training programme has been introduced, including both business training and environmental training to enable them to fulfil the charter.

The members have responded well to the environmental orientation of the Association and is believed that this is one of the main reasons for commitment to it and a growth in its membership.

The Association has taken on most of the marketing functions of the Tarka Project, including producing their own guide, publicity and handling enquiries.

As with most bodies of this kind, the work has had to fall upon a few dedicated individuals, who put in their time for free, though their expenses can be met by the Tarka Project. To encourage membership, subscriptions were kept low (£5–£10 initially, now raised to £25). This may lead to problems in the future, if the Association really is to be self-financing and have an impact. To date it has had to rely on the Project for much of its support. The Association is now at a critical stage if it is to develop into a strong, active body. A Development Plan has been prepared which seeks for public sector funding to take it through this stage, assisted by a development officer, and including membership and revenue targets as well as a realistic action programme. If it is able to follow this route, the Association should provide a long term, sustainable mechanism for taking forward the achievements and approach of the Tarka Project.

The tourist association has taken forward the Tarka logo and branding. © Tarka Project.

A chef using a green cone digester in South Devon. © South Devon Green Tourism Initiative.

Helping enterprises adopt sustainable management practices

The overall experience of the projects, as identified above, is that rural tourism enterprises are quite interested in environmental issues but don't give them a high priority. This was confirmed by some research undertaken for the South Devon Green Tourism Initiative. Some of the projects have tried specifically to encourage and enable enterprises to turn this interest into practice in their own operations.

The Dartmoor Area Tourism Initiative mailed a *Green business guide* to enterprises throughout their area, with simple tips and suggestions, although there was relatively little interest in this. They also ran an environmental award scheme, as have the North Pennines partnership and Project Explore. The Tarka Project established a Green Charter as a condition of membership of the tourist association.

The greatest amount of work in this area has been carried out by the South Devon Initiative, which has been a focused pilot project testing a particular technique — a self-administered *Green Audit Kit*. This was found to be successful and is being taken forward nationally.

Lessons learnt include the following:
- Tourism enterprises will respond to green concepts if these are properly set out and they are clearly shown how to go about it. Pointing out the cost savings that can be made is the best way of attracting interest.
- The South Devon approach, of encouraging people to take simple steps slowly and consistently along a path and to be recognised and applauded for what they are doing, appears to be the right one.
- Simply mailing guides to enterprises does not work. A more personal and in depth approach is needed.
- Green Charters can be helpful in setting out what groups of businesses are trying to do and putting this over to the public, but they lead to false expectations if they are not fulfilled. They need to be backed up by training and advice.
- Green awards can be helpful. Two types might be pursued:
  - An annual prize for innovation or hard work, perhaps administered locally. This is easy to handle, provides some incentive and is good for PR and demonstration purposes.
  - A scheme of identifying enterprises which have reached a certain environmental standard, and which the public can recognise - essentially green labelling. This needs more care and should be coordinated nationally.

The outcome of all this in terms of what enterprises have actually done has been mixed, but steps have been taken in the right direction. A number of positive examples have been recorded in South Devon (see box on page 46).

The overall conclusion from the South Devon Initiative was that the *Green Audit Kit* should be amended and made available nationally. It was recognised that ideally some support and training backup should be provided. An approach recommended from the Initiative was to seek to establish groups of enterprises in local areas, who would receive initial training and then work together on implementing the kit, aiding and encouraging each other, with occasional checkups and prompting.

Small steps to going green

The following are some of the small steps taken by tourism enterprises in South Devon who are using the *Green Audit Kit* developed by the Green Tourism Initiative.

- Installing low energy light bulbs, especially in places lit for long periods. This is the favourite first step. Plymouth Personal Service, a network of 35 guesthouses, have negotiated a bulk purchase for members of these light bulbs, mitigating any additional cost involved.
- Informing visitors. Some hotels have introduced notice boards with information on local sites, or placed 'green files' in bedrooms with personally collected information on places to visit. Guest house owners and hotel staff are talking more knowledgeably to their visitors about the local environment. Full public transport information is increasingly provided.
- Composting organic waste. Various methods have been used, including wormeries. Establishments with gardens are using compost to produce fresh organic vegetables.
- Reducing waste in bathrooms. Use of liquid soaps is becoming more common. The Royal Castle Hotel, Dartmouth, reduced towel use, by asking guests to indicate that they want them washed by placing them in the bath (though by getting the wording wrong to start with it initially had the opposite effect).
- Separating various waste products and recycling more items.

Green Audit Kit

The *Green Audit Kit* was prepared by the South Devon Green Tourism Initiative as a self-help manual for tourism enterprises.

The kit was written by the project manager in close consultation with local businesses, testing out ideas and producing various drafts. It was produced as a loose leaf folder so that pages could be photocopied, people could add their own bits and updates could be bound in to reflect technical changes. Separate sections covered: energy, transport, purchasing, waste, health and conserving the local environment. Each section included:

- an information sheet, explaining the issues and how to tackle them;
- an audit sheet, for users to fill in to record what they had done; and
- an action sheet, which showed, through symbols, the relative benefits of different actions in terms of overheads, costs, payback and environmental benefits.

Special attention was paid to the appearance of the kit, using a professional designer. The bold front cover and use of colours and graphics inside was found to be particularly successful in attracting attention to it, arousing interest and encouraging people to use it. The kit was given a cover price of £3.50, so people would value it but not be put off from buying it. Subsequent research suggested that it could have borne a higher price.

Environmental consultants, funded jointly by the Countryside Commission and Rural Development Commission, to assess the kit, found a high level of satisfaction amongst purchasers, but concluded that it should contain more practical guidance on actually how to take action. This was generally accepted. A revised version of the kit is now being prepared for use nationally.

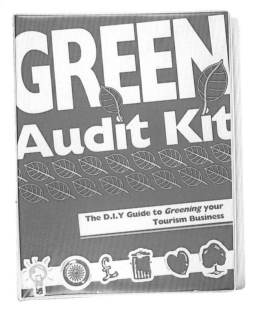

Awareness of the Green Audit Kit was helped by a strong cover design.

3. THE CASE STUDY PROJECTS

This chapter takes a detailed look at 15 of the more comprehensive case study projects taken from the 21 projects, in total, that were examined.

These are:

- Project Explore, Cornwall.
- Devon and Cornwall Rail Partnership.
- Purbeck Heritage Committee, Dorset.
- Dartmoor Area Tourism Initiative.
- Peak Tourism Partnership.
- Surrey Hills Visitor Project.
- Wiltshire Downs Project.
- Tarka Project, Devon.
- North Pennines Tourism Partnership.
- South Somerset District Council.
- Lake District Traffic Management Initiative.
- South Devon Green Tourism Initiative.
- Settle and Carlisle Railway Development Company.
- Norfolk Coast Project.
- Nightingale Project, Kent.

The case study summaries have been compiled by examining written material, visiting the areas and carrying out in depth interviews with the project managers, and talking to other participants in the process. For each case study we discuss:

- The context and background.
- Origins and objectives.
- Organisation, staffing and funding.
- The general approach taken.
- An overview of the various initiatives pursued (some are written up in more detail in the boxes in Chapter 2).
- Plans for the future.
- Our overall assessment of what the project has achieved and the lessons to be learned.

Project Explore — Green tourism in South–east Cornwall

Project Explore is an initiative between local interests and agencies aimed at encouraging the development of green tourism in South–east Cornwall.

Location:	South East Cornwall (Looe, Polperro, Liskeard)
Partners:	Countryside Commission, West Country Tourist Board, Cornwall County Council, Caradon District Council, Cornwall Wildlife Trust, town and parish councils, South East Cornwall Tourism Association, Cornwall Tourism Development Action Programme (year 1), South Cornwall Heritage Coast Service (phase 1), Restmoral District Council (phase 2).
Structure:	Steering group, full time project manager.
Timescale:	Phase 1 July 1991 – March 1993 Phase 2 April 1993 – March 1996
Core Funding:	£44,000 annual average (1991– 1995)

Points of interest:
- creation of a visitor centre to influence visitors.
- involvement of local community organisations.
- small scale initiatives to broaden the tourism appeal.
- use of events and festivals.
- integrated with countryside management service.

Using Punch and Judy at Looe to get across green messages.
© *Project Explore.*

Context

Project Explore covers some 90 sq miles of coast and countryside between Looe and Fowey in South–east Cornwall. This is an attractive area with a rugged coast and beautiful countryside, including both heritage coast and Area of Outstanding Natural Beauty. Tourism is an important sector of the economy but traditionally has a short season and is concentrated on the coast.

Origins and objectives

The Looe Action Plan of 1988 first suggested making more of the surrounding countryside as a tourism resource. A consultancy report in 1990, *An encouragement to explore*, suggested how the area could be marketed and interpreted, particularly to encourage off-peak tourism. Project Explore was set up to take forward the report recommendations. Caradon District Council and the South Cornwall Heritage Coast Service were instrumental in setting up the project.

The aim of the project was 'to promote and develop tourism which is based on the character of the area, its beauty, culture and wildlife and with emphasis on developing tourism outside the peak holiday months'.

Objectives:
- Improving information, interpretation and access to the countryside
- Involving the local community in implementation
- Demonstrating the positive relationship between tourism and the environment
- Ensuring successful long term management of the area

Project Explore concentrated on reaching visitors already in the area whilst the tourism officer for Caradon District Council focused on promoting South–east Cornwall outside the area. A close working relationship between the officers has minimised overlap and conflict.

Organisation and funding

A steering group, which meets quarterly, consists of 11 officers and members from the County and District, town and parish councils, Cornwall Trust for Nature Conservation, Countryside Commission, West Country Tourist Board and the local tourist association.

There is a full-time project officer based at the Discovery Centre in Looe. Since 1993 the officer has been responsible for both the Countryside Service and the Centre, resulting in another one and a half posts. Caradon District Council acts as the employer and provides the office.

Financial summary:

Average annual core budget (1992–1995) £44,000

Income:		
	Countryside Commission	34%
	English Tourist Board/	
	West Country Tourist Board	8%
	Local Authorities	33%
	Parish Councils/	
	Town Councils	6%
	Other	19%
Expenditure:	Staff/admin	54%
	Projects	46%

The project has been very successful at generating funding for green tourism initiatives from other sources with an additional £258,000 being spent on initiatives set up or coordinated under the umbrella of Project Explore in the period 1991–1994.

Approach

The 1990 report provided a ready-made strategy full of ideas which formed the basis of the work programme in the first two years. This made for a quick start. Considerable emphasis has been placed on developing initiatives in consultation with local people and local organisations. Whilst this is time consuming it has been crucial in establishing local support.

Initiatives undertaken

Information provision

The most visible project, identified in the 1990 report, has been the development of the South–east Cornwall Discovery Centre. This is located in the main visitor car park in West Looe encouraging visitors to explore the countryside, heritage and culture of the area. The centre includes a shop, information centre, exhibition and toilets and was funded by Caradon District Council with assistance from the European Union, Rural Development Commission and Countryside Commission. The project officer played a key role in the design and setting up of the centre, later taking responsibility for its management (see box on page 41).

Information panels and pedestrian signposting schemes have been designed and put in place in Looe and Liskeard. These have provided early visible evidence of the project and have been widely welcomed by both towns. Leaflets were produced giving local information on cycling and fishing.

Interpretation of heritage interest

In addition to the exhibition in the Discovery Centre, a number of leaflets have been produced interpreting local churches, village and town trails and the Liskeard and Looe Union Canal. There is great enthusiasm amongst local groups for producing them, although because print runs are small (less than 5,000 copies) the project officer has some doubts as to their effectiveness.

Public transport initiatives

Project Explore participates in the Looe Valley Line Working Party (see Devon and Cornwall Rail Partnership) producing the popular line guide leaflet and an insert of train and bus services. Passenger levels on the line increased by ten per cent in 1994. The Bodmin-Lostwithiel project was also helped to devise boat and bus excursions on the River Fowey and passenger excursions on the mineral line between Lostwithiel and Fowey.

Access to the countryside

A major project was the purchase of Trenant Woods at Looe by the Woodland Trust in 1991–1992, to enhance public access. Project Explore played a significant part in preparing the case to secure funding. Since 1993, the project officer also manages the local countryside service and this has enabled a closer integration of green tourism initiatives and countryside management schemes.

Events

An extensive programme of events and guided walks is arranged. These are publicised through a commercial leaflet drop to pubs and accommodation. Additional coverage is through Cornwall County Councils Green Guide and Caradon District Council's own newspaper. Events are popular but attended mainly by the converted. To try reaching a wider audience a beach puppet show was staged in 1994 with a strong green message about litter. Bad weather spoiled its potential.

In the 1993 Spring half term Project Explore coordinated a major community festival 'Looe & Polperro: Festival of the Sea', which included a week long programme of events. Stories and reminiscences were collected of life in the old fishing ports. The plan is to make this a regular event although it has proved difficult to find people to take on the organisation.

Other activities

Significant effort was put into raising awareness of the project and of green tourism in general. This included production of a leaflet, presentations to local groups and obtaining media coverage. Workshops were held for tourism operators and tourist information centre staff to introduce them to the Discovery Centre and the Looe Valley Line. A successful leaflet swop shop was held for local tourism businesses.

A green tourism award has been established in association with Caradon District Council, coupled with small grant scheme to stimulate projects.

The future

The project will continue to 1996. Current work includes cycle route guides, village information points and farm tourism workshops. The long term future of the project is uncertain despite wide support, one option being incorporation into a proposed European Union LEADER programme.

Assessment

Project Explore has attracted wide support, proving to be an effective mechanism for getting local interests and agencies to work together. In the process it has expanded horizons, raised awareness of green tourism and initiated a large number of small scale projects aimed at improving the visitors' experience.

It is difficult to ascertain impact on the visitors, and is perhaps best seen as the start of a process to broaden the nature of tourism in the area. Apart from a useful survey of visitors to the Discovery Centre there has been relatively little enthusiasm for monitoring, partly because of the difficulty of measuring the impact of small scale projects.

Particular achievements

- The creation of the Discovery Centre. This is a visible and popular facility attracting 100,000 visitors a year. It is a flagship for Project Explore, raising its profile amongst visitors and locals, as well as increasing awareness of the surrounding area.
- Enriching the tourism product. A combination of better information provision and small scale initiatives has improved the range of activities and opportunities open to visitors. There is now more to see and do in the area and a more substantial product to market for off-peak holidays.

- Breaking down barriers. The project has been instrumental in bringing local communities and agencies together and developing a fruitful partnerships. The project has very strong local commitment and support.
- A greater awareness of green tourism. Tourism in the area has traditionally been dominated by the resorts and the coast. There is now a greater local awareness of the potential of the countryside and the need for a sensitive approach.
- Generating funding for green tourism projects. In addition to its direct funds it has played an important role in levering additional funding for tourism projects to enabling them to proceed.

Some lessons and pointers

- Local involvement is critical to gaining acceptance and ensuring initiatives are continued, but it is time consuming and wearing process. There is also a danger of resources being spread too thinly on low key projects with limited impact.
- It is hard work securing the commitment and involvement of the local tourism industry. Many small operators are fighting for survival and are not able or interested in taking a wider view, many are simply amateurs. Improving professionalism and raising standards in the local tourism industry is a major challenge.
- It is important to generate evidence of success to gain credibility. The Discovery Centre has played a significant part along with the pedestrian signposting schemes in Looe and Liskeard.
- Operating within just one district council area makes things very much simpler to organise.

The Devon and Cornwall Rail Partnership — On the right lines

A project to encourage greater leisure use of the rural rail network in Devon and Cornwall.

Location:	Devon and Cornwall
Partners:	Countryside Commission, Rural Development Commission, Regional Railways, Cornwall County Council, Devon County Council, University of Plymouth, Cornwall Tourism Development Action Programme, (stage 2 only) Dartmoor National Park, Plymouth City Council
Structure:	Steering group of sponsors, officer group and line working groups. Full time project officer and secretarial support.
Timescale:	Phase 1 July 1991 – July 1994 Phase 2 July 1994 – July 1997
Core funding:	£32,000 annual average (1992–1994) £43,000 annual average (1994–1997)

Points of interest:
- Public transport marketing.
- Monitoring of use and impacts.
- Linking rural railways to countryside recreation opportunities.
- Involving local interests in improving and developing lines.

Context

Eight rural branch lines in Devon and Cornwall run from the main London to Penzance line to the coast. Single track lines, they follow river valleys and pass through beautiful countryside providing access to attractive small towns and resorts. They were instrumental in opening up Devon and Cornwall to tourism in the 19th and early 20th century. Today, encouraging their leisure use will help ensure their survival.

Origins and objectives

Regional Railways and Devon County Council have collaborated for some time to increase the viability of these rural branch lines. Initially work focused on the Tamar Line and the Exeter to Barnstaple Line (Tarka Line) gradually bringing in other partners. The success of these initiatives led to the extension of this approach across Devon and Cornwall.

The aim of the Partnership was 'to encourage greater use of the two counties' rural railways for leisure and recreation — not only by visitors, but also by local residents'.

Objectives were to:
- Improve access to rural areas for leisure and recreation.
- Improve the long term viability of rural transport for social and economic reasons.
- Encourage sustainable tourism by reducing private car use and limiting the impact of visitors on the local environment.
- Bring additional economic benefits to communities served by the rural rail network.
- Benefit local and distant populations by developing rural areas as a leisure resource.

Organisation and funding

An initial steering group consisted of Devon County Council, Cornwall County Council, Countryside Commission, Rural Development Commission, Regional Railways, University of Plymouth and the Cornwall Tourist Development Action Programme (first year only) with Countryside Commission and University of Plymouth playing the major roles. It was later extended to include Dartmoor National Park and Plymouth City Council with the Rural Development Commission and University taking an active role. It contains both officers and members and meets every six months.

An officer group is responsible for implementation and guides the work of the partnership officer. Working groups exist for six of the lines bringing together local interests, particularly local authorities. These generate funds and progress projects in their own areas with the support of the partnership officer. These groups meet six monthly.

The Partnership is staffed by a full-time officer plus secretarial support, and since 1995 a part time assistant. An office is provided by the University of Plymouth.

Financial summary:		
Average annual core budget (1992–1994) £32,000		
Income:	Local authorities	36%
	Countryside Commission	27%
	Rural Development Commission	15%
	Regional Railways	6%
	University of Plymouth	13%
	Other	4%
Expenditure:	Staff/admin	81%
	Projects	19%

Core funding covers the central costs plus a small amount for pump priming projects and research. This has increased in phase 2. Most of the actual expenditure on improvement and promotion of the lines has been raised on a line by line basis from 27 local partners, plus the European Union and British Rail Community Fund. For example £56,000 was spent on the Tamar Valley Line (1991–1993) on publicity and infrastructure works.

Approach

The aim has been to mobilise local interest and enthusiasm on a line by line basis with overall direction and support from the project. Work concentrated initially on the Tarka, Tamar valley and Looe Valley lines, later spreading to the St Ives line and the Bodmin Steam Railway. Work has now included the Newquay Branch Line and the Truro to Falmouth Line.

A passenger leisure survey was carried out in 1992 by the University of Plymouth. This coupled with BR passenger figures showed the project's impact. Further surveys are planned using self completion questionnaires distributed in the Line Guides.

Initiatives undertaken

Station enhancements and signing

Improvements have been made to signing, facilities and the overall appearance of stations. Examples include pedestrian signing at Looe and Barnstaple, a new walkway and lighting at Crediton, environmental improvements at Barnstaple, and redecoration at Liskeard.

Links from the railway

Walking and cycling links from the stations into the surrounding countryside have been created to encourage use of the lines by selling a rail based countryside experience, not just a ticket. Leaflets have promoted walks and cycle facilities from Eggesford Station on the Tarka line and circular walks from stations along the

A special excursion train opens up the Fowey Valley freight line to visitors. © Paul Watts Photography/Devon & Cornwall Rail Partnership.

Tamar Valley Line. Bus links, highlighted in special supplements to the line guides on the Tarka and Looe Valley Line, encourage wider exploration. Special Sunday bus services have been introduced to give access from the Tamar Valley Line to Dartmoor, opening up 300 miles of rural bus routes.

Promotion and interpretation

The Partnership produces a guide to the rural rail network, *Explore Devon and Cornwall*. This a full colour, folded A2 sized leaflet, and is produced in large quantities (280,000 pa). This is the main vehicle for promotion. Supported by advertising and press work it is distributed both within the area and at key locations beyond including mainline stations and on Cross Country Inter City Holiday Maker trains through Birmingham.

Full colour folded A3 sized line guides are produced for the Tarka, Tamar Valley and Looe Valley Lines, giving details of routes and places of interest. Produced in more limited quantities (70,000) they are distributed within the region through tourist information centres, accommodation, libraries and BR outlets. Timetable inserts also give details of services and connections. Laminated timetable posters have been produced for pubs and shops.

Interpretive panels at stations give details of walks and features of interest. A 32 page Adventure Pack has been produced for the Tarka Line (2,000 copies) providing activities, puzzles and interest for children and families, free for purchasers of a family ticket.

Education packs have been produced for the St Ives and Looe Valley Line.

Community involvement

The partnership has involved the local community and acted as a liaison between communities and the railway, raising local interest and commitment to the lines. Examples include a successful Victorian Day launching the Looe Valley Line Project and The Tamar Travellers Community Project. The latter was an imaginative arts event, involving some 130 people and linking two rural and two urban communities connected by the Tamar Line.

Recreational Packages

Various experiments have tested rail based recreation packages. A summer charter on the Fowey–Lostwithiel freight line was organised over four days in 1994. Guided walks and events have been organised from stations on the Tamar Valley Line with the local countryside service, including combined river/rail trips. A new Sunday service on the Tamar Line used information assistants on the train, linked to a new network of bus services from Gunnislake. Ticket holders received discounts at attractions.

Enhanced facilities

The partnership has supported other facilities, for example a cycle hire business at Barnstaple Station, attracting 16,500 customers in just over three years, and an interpretation centre for the Tarka line based in a garden centre at Egglesford. Passengers to Egglesford increased by some 20 per cent (1992–1993) as a result of its promotion as a countryside destination.

The future

The Partnership has been extended to 1997 with new partners and increased resources. The plan is to continue existing initiatives, extend to other lines, and explore ways of increasing the impact of the rural railways and raise awareness of their importance.

Assessment

This important and well focused project has transformed views about the rural rail network amongst elected members, officers and local communities, coming at a time of growing interest in public transport and sustainability. The rural rail network is now seen as a significant asset for the region rather than as an outmoded legacy of the past. The partnership has also successfully mobilised the support of local agencies and communities.

It has ably demonstrated the impact of its activities in terms of increased passenger levels and this has been persuasive in attracting support. More could have been done to investigate the effectiveness of the various line publicity leaflets, although future surveys should accomplish this.

Rail privatisation has caused some problems by splitting the responsibilities between Rail Track and Regional Railways and making communication and cooperation more difficult. In this context the Partnership has a vital role to play in helping develop new strategies and improving communication.

Particular achievements

- Physical improvements to services and stations and better information.
- Increased use of the rural rail network. The Tamar Valley Line has increased passengers by around seven per cent pa (1991–1994) whilst the Looe valley Line has shown a substantial lengthening of the peak season, showing a ten per cent increase in passengers between 1992–1993 and 1994.
- Reducing the environmental impact of visitors. Research suggests around half the respondents on the Tamar, Tarka and Looe lines could have come by car. 25 per cent were using the train to avoid parking problems and traffic.
- Bringing economic benefits to communities served by the rail network. An estimated £0.5m was generated in Looe by the Looe Valley Line in 1992–1993.

Some lessons and pointers

- Beware of creating too cumbersome a structure. There is a danger that the project officer can become bogged down in servicing committees. Project officers need administrative support.
- Focusing on something specific like a railway line is a good way of capturing people's interest and imagination, but remember to promote the whole public transport package including bus links and countryside destinations.
- Outcomes that are measurable make it easier to justify support. Monitoring and surveys are important in providing hard evidence to gauge the impacts of these projects.

The Purbeck Heritage Committee — Keeping Purbeck special

Purbeck Heritage Committee is a partnership of local agencies and interests set up to coordinate a strategy for protecting the character and environment of Purbeck and promoting sustainable development.

Location:	Isle of Purbeck, Dorset
Partners:	Countryside Commission, English Nature, Southern Tourist Board, Dorset County Council, Purbeck District Council, accommodation operators, Country Landowners Assoc., National Farmers Union, National Trust, town and parish councils.
Structure:	Purbeck Heritage Committee oversees project. Purbeck Forum provides mechanism for wider discussion and consultation. Officer steering group. Full time project officer.
Timescale:	1993–2000.
Core funding:	£29,000 annual average (1993–1995)

Points of interest:
- Extensive consultation, community involvement and consensus building.
- Mobilising resources of existing agencies and organisations.
- Effective use of consultants as advisers and facilitators.
- Visitor management projects and environmental improvement projects.
- Public transport improvements based around private railway.
- Relationship of seaside resort to rural hinterland.

Context

Purbeck in the south of Dorset includes both an Area of Outstanding Natural Beauty and Heritage Coast. As well as a striking coastline, it has a rich diversity of landscape, wildlife, historic sites and attractive towns and villages. It is a traditional holiday area, originally focused on the seaside resort of Swanage, but also drawing day visitors from nearby Bournemouth, Poole and Weymouth. About 4.5 million visitor days are spent in the area each year. Visitor pressure is causing problems in terms of traffic congestion, footpath erosion and threats to wildlife.

Origins and objectives

The Purbeck Heritage Committee was formed in 1993 after an extensive period of debate about environmental problems facing Purbeck. This took place at local authority member level, involved both district and county councils, the Southern Tourist Board and Countryside Commission, and was stimulated by a consultant's report of 1991 which looked at visitor management in the area. The lengthy period of debate was essential in building political support and consensus with the consultant retained as advisor throughout.

As a result, the Heritage Committee was created as an independent body to oversee the production of a strategy and action plan for the Purbeck Heritage Area. It brought together relevant interests and was set up for an initial period of two years, subsequently extended to the year 2000. Its independence from the district council was important in establishing credibility and support.

The Committee was charged with developing a strategy which would:
- Coordinate action on conservation and countryside management.
- Encourage more appropriate forms of tourism.
- Reduce dependency on the private car.

The Committee acted as coordinator and catalyst rather than undertaking initiatives itself. Although participation in the Committee implied that the partners were willing to support and help fund the initiatives identified.

Organisation and funding

The Purbeck Heritage Committee has a formal constitution and 19 members and officers nominated by the county and district council, Countryside Commission, Southern Tourist Board, Country Landowners' Association, National Farmers' Union, Dorset Association of Town and Parish Councils, English Nature, National Trust and the Swanage & District, Hotel, Guest House & Self Catering Association. It meets quarterly and has an independent chairman nominated by the Countryside Commission.

The Purbeck Forum provides an opportunity for a much wider range of interests to contribute to the initiative and brings together some 94 community based, conservation, tourism and interest groups. This body meets to discuss issues and establish priorities for the strategy. Workshops facilitated by outside consultants were used to aid this process.

An officer steering group, on which the Heritage Committee Chairman sits, meets as required and works with the project officer to coordinate, develop and implement initiatives. This group reports back progress to the full committee. A project officer, appointed February 1994, works from Purbeck District Council offices.

Unlike many projects there is no dedicated budget for the initiative apart from the costs of the project officer, amounting to £29,000 pa. This is funded by Purbeck District Council (50 per cent), Countryside Commission (40 per cent), Dorset County Council (10 per cent). In addition, each partner has made substantial resources available to fund specific initiatives. For example, the District Council committed £300,000 towards the Swanage seafront and pier and £90,000 towards car parking improvements in Corfe. Bids have also been made for funding from other sources.

The approach

The project officer drafted the strategy with the various partners. This was important to build her credibility and develop local commitment to the strategy.

The strategy has three main strands – environment, tourism and transport with a series of projects, policies and action points for each.

Responsibility for action rests with the individual agencies. The Committee, working through the project officer and officer steering group, presses for early implementation, coordinates action, raises resources and keeps people informed. A newsletter (*Purbeck View*) has been produced and a 'Purbeck Aware Weekend' held (see box on page 33) to raise peoples' awareness of local environmental issues.

Initiatives undertaken

The strategy has just been published but embraces work which is already under way in a number of areas.

A project is underway to improve the run down seafront in Swanage including restoration of the pier, a heritage centre, new paving and street furniture, lighting, landscaping and planting. A separate officer manages this scheme as part of a wider strategy to regenerate the resort.

At Corfe Castle, new facilities have been created to ease the traffic congestion. A new car and coach park created to the north of the village contains a visitor centre and cafe. The Swanage Railway has been extended from Swanage and a new station created at Norden to the north of Corfe Castle with park and ride facilities and footpaths to the village. Together with signing and changes to village car parks this will reduce traffic levels through the village (see box on page 27). The Purbeck Cycleway, launched in June 1994 and promoted by a colour leaflet, consists of three routes around Purbeck signed along quiet country lanes. In addition four gateway visitor centres are to be created to inform and direct visitors and raise their awareness about the area. The first will open at the Castle View centre in Corfe Castle.

Consultants have been appointed to draw up a tourism marketing plan for the area aimed to develop a thriving tourism economy compatible with the environmental constraints.

A range of other projects are under consideration. The reintroduction of a steamer service between Swanage, Bournemouth and Weymouth. Discussions with the Weld Estate are examining how congestion, parking and erosion problems at Lulworth Cove can be tackled. A package bid has been put together for the Department of Transport for a coordinated set of traffic management measures. An aquatic management plan for Poole harbour has been created to ease conflict between different recreation users and the environment.

The Park and Ride service at Corfe Castle encourages people to leave their cars behind. © Roger Bamber.

The future

The work of the Purbeck Heritage Committee has since been extended until 2000.

Assessment

It is still too early to judge overall impact. Nevertheless it has demonstrated effectiveness at bringing together a wide range of interests, harnessing their enthusiasm and developing a coherent way forward. The strategy is rather general but it does form a useful organisational framework justifying existing projects and new proposals.

The project differs in having no independent funding to undertake initiatives, relying on the participating agencies for funds. This seems to work well so far and the existence of the Heritage Committee has given the proposals a greater weight and higher priority.

Particular achievements

- An integrated approach to tackling pressing and intransigent problems in Swanage and Corfe Castle. These initiatives may ultimately have happened anyway but the project has given them new momentum.
- The selective and controlled use of consultants to supplement local skills and expertise and to act as independent facilitators.
- Local consultation. There has been a strong commitment to consultation and involvement at all levels to build support.

Some lessons and pointers

- Involving elected local authority members is key to gaining support. This is time consuming and extends the process but makes a significant difference eventually to mobilising resources.
- Working within only one District and one County Council area simplifies the process enormously although outside support and resources have been crucial.
- Dealing with problems in a geographically contained and coherent area makes more sense to people and makes for easier communication.
- A high profile committee with a clear brief and formal status can be an effective mechanism for getting things moving.

The Dartmoor Area Tourism Initiative — Naturally beautiful holidays

An initiative to relieve and manage visitor pressure in a National Park through raising awareness of environmental issues and promoting recreation opportunities beyond the park boundary.

Location:	Dartmoor, South Devon
Partners:	Countryside Commission, English Tourist Board, West Country Tourist Board, Dartmoor National Park, Devon County Council, South Hams District Council, Teignbridge District Council, West Devon Borough Council, Dartmoor Tourist Association, Duchy of Cornwall.
Structure:	Steering group providing overall direction. Working groups on projects and marketing. Full time project manager, project officer and secretarial support.
Timescale:	April 1991 – March 1994
Core funding:	£77,000 annual average

Points of interest:
- Working with the local tourist association.
- Using interpretation to divert visitor pressure.
- Influencing coach drivers.
- Local producers group.
- Use of childrens' pack to get message across.
- 'Green' awards and 'green' visitor and business guides.

Context

Dartmoor National Park in South Devon is an area of beautiful and wild countryside consisting of high open moorland, steep wooded river valleys, rolling countryside and picturesque villages. Tourism is a significant and growing part of the local economy. The Park attracts an estimated ten million visits a year, 70 per cent from nearby population centres such as Torbay and Plymouth. Whilst visitor pressures are causing problems at a few locations in the National Park many areas immediately adjoining the Park would welcome more visitors.

Origins and objectives

The Dartmoor Area Tourism Initiative built on the work of a local Tourism Action Programme that had been running in the area for two years. This covered the same area but had a narrower focus and relatively few resources. Although its impact was relatively limited it convinced the participants of the benefits of working together.

The West Country Tourist Board and the Dartmoor National Park put together a new proposal to secure funding from the national agencies and the project was established in 1991.

The aim was to relieve pressures on the National Park by managing visitors in the wider area through a combination of marketing and development work.

The objectives of the project were to:
- Ensure that tourism development reflects the character of the area.
- Divert tourism pressure to the surrounding areas.
- Allow economic benefits to spread into those areas that can absorb increased pressure.
- Manage visitor pressures to reduce impact on local communities and the environment.
- Raise the contribution tourism makes to the local economy.
- Convince the local tourism industry that the approach makes sense.
- Establish its effectiveness.

Organisation and funding

Ten sponsors contributed to the core budget, comprising regional and national tourist boards, Countryside Commission, district and county councils, Dartmoor National Park, Dartmoor Tourist Association and Duchy of Cornwall.

A steering group (20 strong) was formed from representatives of all the above bodies with both officer and member representation. This met every three months to oversee the project.

Two further working groups concerned with projects and marketing met on a three monthly basis. Other ad hoc groups were formed as and when needed to pursue specific initiatives. With hindsight, the size of the steering group and number of management groups was cumbersome, adding to communication problems and causing a significant administrative burden.

The project was staffed by a full time project manager, project officer and secretary. In the first year the original project manager left and this caused some slippage. The project was based at its own office in Princetown provided by the National Park.

The tourism industry were represented on the project through the tourist association. There was no formal community representation although Parish Councils were kept informed of progress throughout. This resulted in very little interest or feedback.

Financial summary:
Average annual core budget:(1991–1994) £77,000

Income:		
English Tourist Board	21%
Countryside Commission	15%
Dartmoor National Park	18%
Local authorities	29%
Dartmoor Tourist Association	4%
Other	13%
Expenditure: Staff/admin	70%
Projects	30%

The core funding for the project was supplemented by £26,000 allocated to specific tasks by the sponsors. European Union funding was also available in the Plymouth Travel to Work Area. This proved hard to spend as it was only available for capital projects in a small area.

Approach

The outline strategy was worked up in more detail by the project manager in consultation with the sponsors. Many of the initiatives had already been identified in an Interpretation Strategy, prepared previously by the National Park. The implementation of this was seen as a key role for the project.

A feature of the project was that it covered 700 sq miles as opposed to the 370 sq miles within the National Park. This provided an opportunity to divert visitor pressure to less sensitive areas spreading economic benefits more widely. The Dartmoor National Park alone were unable to take this wider view of visitor management being restricted to operating within Park boundaries.

Initiatives undertaken

Marketing

Marketing of the Dartmoor area had been patchy and fragmented with little coordination between the tourist association, National Park and local authorities. The project coordinated marketing in this wider area.

The project established an information service dealing with some 2,000–3,000 enquiries a year, half relating to accommodation. They experimented with a computerised accommodation booking system although problems arose getting enterprises to notify availability.

Some 250 purpose designed leaflet display racks were distributed to libraries, information centres and accommodation establishments to raise the awareness of what the area had to offer. Emphasis was placed on exposure in the local media to reach and inform the mainly local visitors.

The project worked closely with the Dartmoor Area Tourist Association to avoid duplicating marketing activity. A recruitment campaign led by the project resulted in a doubling of membership. The Association guide was redesigned to cover the wider area and incorporated the National Park's accommodation list for the first time. Distribution was improved and given more exposure through press trips and articles.

Working with the Association was not easy. Enterprises were suffering from the effects of the recession and were desperate for more business. Many operators would have preferred a more aggressive marketing campaign based on the well known attractions rather than the more sensitive approach favoured by the project.

The project also publicised the project through press launches, newsletters and presentations. This was time consuming and made more difficult by the size of the area and confusion arising from the overlap with other projects such as Tarka.

Public transport

Two initiatives were undertaken to reduce the impact of traffic in the area. A coach drivers handbook was produced and circulated giving suggested tours, encouraging drivers to visit areas outside the moor as well as the moor itself, and putting over a caring message. This was well received by coach operators and appears to have had positive results. The handbook has been adopted by the National Park (see box on page 42).

All publications promoted use of public transport. In addition some 10,000 copies of a publication aimed at the independent visitor, *Next stop please*, was produced. This lists the range of recreational opportunities that are accessible by train and bus. Its use has not been evaluated.

The 'Dartmoor Area Producers' group was given a special launch.
© *Dartmoor Tourism Initiative.*

Work with local producers and farmers

A local producers group 'Dartmoor Area Producers' including food, drink and craft producers, was established following an open meeting attended by 70 people. As a result the group attended craft fairs and produced 5,000 copies of a report featuring 50 producers. It has proved difficult to turn this into a self sustaining initiative. Groups require a lot of hand holding to become established and are critically dependent on there being people with energy, enthusiasm and organisational skills.

Three pilot projects were identified to develop small scale visitor attractions on working farms based around interpretation, farm walks and teas. The results of these were publicised via three well attended seminars attracting over 200 farmers and generating further interest.

A pilot activity breaks promotion was tried with the local farm holiday group, Devon Farms. This was not a success, generating few enquiries, primarily because of the limited promotional budget.

Sustainable tourism

Initiatives took place to raise awareness of green tourism issues amongst operators and visitors. 2,000 copies of a Green Business Guide were produced, launched with Devon Wildlife Trust, and mailed to local businesses. Subsequent research revealed that whilst some action resulted, follow up work was needed to create a meaningful impact. The *Green Audit Kit* became the focus for more serious work.

A Green Visitor Guide was produced to get the message across to visitors. This was written in a light style, illustrated with cartoons. 10,000 copies were distributed via tourist information centres and accommodation establishments. No monitoring took place. Establishments showed little enthusiasm for promoting and distributing it.

Other initiatives included training seminars and two annual award schemes aimed at encouraging environmental awareness (Moor Care) and customer care (Winning Warmest Welcome). The former attracted relatively little interest and was abandoned. The latter was popular attracting 200 entries and is being continued.

Advice and information

10,000 copies of a leaflet were produced to publicise the large number of events offered by different organisations. An experimental events telephone Hotline was established in 1993, but despite promotion via flyers (1,000) and posters (200), it received only 53 calls.

An interpretive map of the area was produced, *Dartmoor area discovery map*, with 12,000 copies distributed for sale to recover costs.

Other examples of coordination include the production of cycling and special needs packs.

Effective distribution of information has proved a continuing problem, one of the main lessons learned is the need to provide resources for the distribution of print.

Interpretation

Interpretation has been used as a positive tool for visitor management. Two leaflets were produced promoting less visited villages, taking pressure off honeypot villages. *The secret villages of the Dartmoor area* was produced in 1991 and promotes nine villages on the edge of the moor. Clocktowers and Cobblestones (1993) promotes ten villages to the north of the moor. This was done in full consultation with the parish councils and has been adopted by the District Council (see box on page 17).

Nine countryside viewpoints have been identified around the moor and interpreted to explain different aspects of Dartmoor's geology, landscape and agriculture. Two leaflets (6,000 copies) to publicise these and have proved extremely popular.

A children's activity pack was produced to promote conservation messages to young visitors. This contained a game, puzzles and activities all themed around the sensitive nature of the area. This has been adopted by the National Park.

Management of pressure

A management project was undertaken in each year of the project to tackle problems on a particular site. These were largely funded by the National Park concentrating on footpath repairs and diversions.

The future

Since the project finished in 1994, a number of outstanding initiatives have been taken forward by a management group representing seven of the original ten sponsors. This meets three times a year. The National Park provides some staff time to help progress certain initiatives and service this group but resources are limited and progress has been slow. A decision has yet to be taken about the long term future.

Assessment

This has been an ambitious project operating on a broad front and covering a wide area. It has attracted wide support, resulted in closer working and coordination between the agencies and tourism interests, and has raised awareness of how tourism can be managed.

The project might have achieved even more by concentrating on slightly fewer initiatives and developing a more streamlined structure. It would also have been helpful, although difficult given the timescale, to have researched the impact of more of the initiatives. Given the origin of most of the day visitors to the National Park, the inclusion of Torbay and Plymouth as partners could have increased the impact of the project.

Particular achievements

- Getting people to work together. As a result of the project there is a greater commitment to joint working. West Devon District Council, Teignbridge District Council, Dartmoor Tourist Association and the National Park are now working on a joint guide and marketing campaign.

- Developing support for tourism management. There is now a greater understanding of the need to manage visitors across the area. Many of the initiatives will continue.
- Extending the tourism product. There is now more information available and awareness of what to see and do.
- Positive attempts to influence visitors and operators. The children's pack, green visitor guide, village leaflets, coach drivers handbook etc have all been useful and innovative initiatives. The impact of these needs to be researched so that they can be refined.

Some lessons and pointers

- Beware of setting up cumbersome bureaucratic structures as it can be time consuming to service and hinders communication.
- It is essential to allow for the costs and mechanics of distribution of print otherwise its effectiveness is much reduced.
- Working with the tourism industry is not easy when dealing with economically fragile, small scale enterprises. Operators are most interested in initiatives which bring an immediate return and are relevant to their operation. Environmental considerations are very much secondary.
- Trying to implement too many initiatives is a drain on resources. Fewer initiatives carried out in greater depth can have greater impact.

The Peak Tourism Partnership — Peak District under pressure

A national pilot project which brought together national agencies and local interests to explore new approaches to managing visitors and tourism in the Peak District.

Location:	The Peak District in Derbyshire, Cheshire, Staffordshire.
Partners:	Countryside Commission, English Nature, English Tourist Board, Rural Development Commission, East Midland Tourist Board, Peak District National Park, Center Parcs, Severn Trent Water, Peak Tourism Forum.
Structure:	Steering group to oversee project. Working groups to pursue specific initiatives. Full time project manager and assistant.
Timescale:	August 1992 – October 1995
Core funding:	£82,000 annual average

Points of interest:
- Integrated visitor management plans for pressure points.
- Strong emphasis on consensus building and community involvement.
- Mechanisms to raise money from visitors for environmental projects.
- Local interpretive plans as a tool for visitor management.
- Focused approach on limited number of projects.
- Use of consultants as facilitators and to develop initiatives.

Context

The Peak Park, straddling the counties of Staffordshire, Cheshire and Derbyshire is the busiest National Park in Europe attracting 22 million visits a year. A high proportion of visitors are people on day trips from the surrounding conurbations attracted by the distinctive scenery and the opportunities for outdoor recreation. Whilst these visitors are important to the local economy they generate problems in terms of traffic congestion, erosion to footpaths, nuisance to farmers and disruption to local communities. These problems are causing increasing concern.

Origins and objectives

Discussions were already underway to establish a tourism initiative in the Peak District to improve joint working and build on the work of the Peak Tourism Forum, a local authority marketing group. With the publication of the Task Force report in 1991, *Tourism and the environment – Maintaining The Balance* it was decided to place more emphasis on sustainable tourism and visitor management and bid for national funding for the initiative. The East Midlands Tourist Board took the lead role in putting the project together.

The Peak Tourism Partnership was established in August 1992 as a national pilot project for a three year period.

Its objectives were to:
- Develop an integrated approach to visitor management
- Increase the local economic benefit from tourism
- Examine means of raising funds from visitors towards conservation and visitor management
- Develop a regional interpretation strategy
- Encourage further collaboration and joint working on tourism particularly with the private sector

Organisation and funding

The project is overseen by an officer steering group nominated by the core funding agencies. This has nine members representing English Tourist Board, East Midlands Tourist Board (representing the four regional tourist boards), Peak National Park, Peak Tourism Forum (representing 11 local authorities), Countryside Commission, Rural Development Commission, English Nature, Severn Trent Water and Centre Parcs, plus two chairmen of the visitor management working groups. It meets three–four times a year, chaired by a Director of the Peak National Park.

Local authorities are represented on the steering group by the Peak Tourism Forum, a long established group set up to coordinate tourism marketing across the Peak District. Representation was restricted because of the large number of local authorities covered by the Peak District. The lack of direct involvement of local authorities, particularly at a member level, has made it more difficult to attract support for implementation.

A series of working groups have been formed to develop and take forward specific initiatives such as the two visitor management plans and the interpretation plans. These have provided an opportunity to involve a broader spread of local authorities, community representatives and private sector interests.

The project was staffed by a project manager, joined in January 1993 by an assistant project officer with additional part-time clerical support from September 1994.

To emphasise the independence of the project an independent project office was established.

The core funding for the project amounted to £82,000 pa. This covered staffing, administration and the costs of minor projects and consultancy. Other funding was raised to take forward specific initiatives. A project to promote the use of the Hope Valley Rail line generated an additional £20,000 and sponsorship for the environment fund a further £15,000. Implementing the various projects is dependent on funding from local authorities and agencies.

Financial summary:

Average annual core budget (1992–1995) £82,000

Income:	English Tourist Board/	
	East Midlands Tourist Board	21%
	Countryside Commission	10%
	Rural Development	
	Commission	20%
	Peak Park & Local	
	Authorities	30%
	Private sector	12%
	Other	7%
Expenditure:	Staff/admin	56%
	Management plans	21%
	Interpretation	11%
	Environment fund	3%
	Marketing	2%
	PR	7%

Approach

An outline strategy and work programme was drawn up by the East Midlands Tourist Board in discussion with the other partners, this was developed in more detail by the project manager under the guidance of the steering group. Six main areas of work were identified.

- Visitor management plans in the Upper Hope Valley and the Roaches.
- An interpretation strategy for the Peak District.
- A heritage trust for securing funding from visitors.
- A Peak District Tourist Association.
- Marketing and developing sustainable tourism.
- Publicising the project.

Work was started on all these areas. Given the short timescale, use was made of a variety of outside consultants to undertake research and develop an approach.

Gradually the project became more focused on visitor management and less so on marketing. It developed a strong commitment to involving local communities in initiatives to ensure that ideas were relevant and increase the likelihood of implementation.

The Partnership saw its role as developing ideas, identifying mechanisms for implementation and funding and then transferring them to local interests.

The project was publicised through a local press launch attended by the National Heritage Minister, media exposure, circulation of regular newsletters, and presentations to local groups. The size of the area made communication difficult.

Initiatives undertaken

Visitor management plans

Visitor management plans were drawn up for two areas in the Peak District experiencing acute problems of visitor pressure; the Roaches in the Staffordshire Moorlands and the Castleton/Hope/Edale area in High Peak, Derbyshire. A key feature of both plans was the way in which the local community and other interests were involved, from identifying issues, appointing consultants and developing a programme of action (see box on page 32).

The two plans put forward an integrated set of proposals costing about £1 million. Recommendations cover traffic management, parking, public transport, information provision, interpretation, recreation management and initiatives for the local tourism industry. The aim in each case is to manage better the numbers of visitors to these areas and modify their impact. The project subsequently concentrated its effort on identifying sources of funding and getting the relevant agencies and local authorities to adopt these plans.

It was felt important to deliver some action in the short term. One successful initiative in 1994 was a promotional campaign to increase the use of the Hope Valley Railway Line linked with an increased Sunday service, shuttle buses and guided walks. This was popular and resulted in passenger levels more than doubling in the summer of 1994. A survey showed that nearly half of these people would have come by car had the train not been available.

Interpretation strategy

An Interpretation Group was formed from people with an interest in interpretation. Consultants were used to facilitate the meetings as an innovative way of producing an interpretative strategy for the wider Peak District. Six pilot areas were then selected for the production of detailed local interpretive plans with the aim of using interpretation to influence visitor behaviour. Each plan was prepared by a specially convened local working group drawing on valuable local knowledge and an interest in pursuing implementation. Consultants were used as facilitators.

Raising funding from visitors

A Peak District wide trust — The Peak District Tourism and Environment Fund — has been established to collect and channel voluntary contributions from visitors to environmental projects. This project

Striking stickers remind visitors of the environment fund. © Peak Tourism Partnership.

originated from an earlier English Tourist Board/ Countryside Commission study and was based on findings from local research which suggested that visitors were receptive to the idea. Two small pilot schemes were established with collecting points in car parks in the Hope Valley and in accommodation outlets throughout the Peak District (see box on page 37). The scheme was launched in August 1994 and in the first nine months collected some £2,000. Sponsorship covered start-up costs.

Marketing and tourism association

Efforts to establish a tourism association and develop a sustainable marketing strategy have proved less successful. There was relatively little interest from the commercial sector in forming a Peak District wide tourism association because operators tend to relate to their local area rather than the Peak District as a whole.

The Partnership sought to influence the long term marketing of the Peak District, particularly by local authorities. A marketing working group was set up involving local authorities and tourism operators. The group produced an outline marketing strategy for the Peak Tourism Forum. Relatively little progress has been made due to a lack of resources and the disruption caused by the Local Government review. The Partnership has funded several individual projects, for example a sustainable marketing seminar and an activity holidays guide.

Assessment

This has been a very focused project which has concentrated its resources on developing and establishing a limited number of innovative pilot schemes. This approach partly reflects the nature of the initiative as a national pilot project charged with testing visitor management techniques. In general, the initiatives undertaken have been well prepared, have produced some useful lessons and are slowly beginning to result in action on the ground.

The project has been less successful in stimulating interest from the local tourism industry and found it difficult to build political support with agencies and local authorities. It is important that the partners make a commitment to implementing and supporting initiatives in the longer term because without this initiatives will falter. Working in a smaller geographical area might have improved communication and increased effectiveness.

Positive achievements

- Local involvement. There has been a deliberate and innovative attempt to involve local communities in the planning and implementation of projects. This can be a long, and at times, painful process but it lies at the heart of sustainable tourism and can pay dividends in terms of bringing people together.
- Moving visitor management up the agenda. There are signs that local authorities and other agencies are incorporating the visitor management plans into their own programmes and strategies. Many of the transport proposals for the Hope Valley were incorporated into the Derbyshire County Council's Package Bid to the Department of Transport.
- New approaches to raising funding from visitors. A mechanism has been put in place for raising additional funding from visitors which will outlast the project. The project has helped advance our understanding of the practicalities of this idea.

Some lessons and pointers

- Too large an area is self defeating. The size and complexity of the study area has made it difficult for the project to generate a high profile across the Peak District as a whole, in the time available.
- Political support is vital. The size of the project and lack of involvement of local councillors at the outset has made it more difficult to win political support for taking initiatives forward. This position has been aggravated by the Local Government review and continuing pressures on local authorities.
- Involving the tourism industry is difficult. Small operators have a short time horizon, and relate to very local areas. Stimulating their interest depends on delivering them something useful.
- Development projects have a long lead time. A short term project can only get proposals to the starting gate. It is critically important to ensure proposals are taken forward after the project finishes.
- It is quite difficult to get substantial projects off the ground in such a short timescale.

The Surrey Hills Visitor Project — Days out in the North Downs

A project aimed at managing visitor pressure and encouraging sustainable tourism in the Surrey Hills Area of Outstanding Natural Beauty.

Location:	Central swathe of Surrey, running east – west across the county.
Partners:	Countryside Commission, English Tourist Board, South East Tourist Board, Surrey County Council, National Trust, Network South East, Thames Trains, (phase 2) Reigate & Banstead Borough Council, Waverley Borough Council, Mole Valley Borough Council.
Structure:	Steering group to oversee project. Full time project Manager.
Timescale:	Phase 1 Sept 1992 – April 1995 Phase 2 April 1995 – April 1997
Core funding:	£43,000 annual average (1992–1995)

Points of interest:
- Visitor management projects on sensitive sites.
- Public transport improvement and promotion.
- Stimulating investment by other agencies.
- Promotion of walking.

Context

Surrey Hills Area of Outstanding Natural Beauty runs east-west across the county and includes the North Downs. A mixture of heath and downland, it embraces picturesque villages and honeypots such as Box Hill and Frensham Ponds. Due to its location and accessibility the area is well used by Surrey residents and Londoners and suffers from some problems of traffic congestion, physical damage and nuisance.

Origins and objectives

The initial idea for the project came from Surrey County Council, partly stimulated by the Government's Task Force report, *Maintaining The Balance*. The idea was supported by the South East England Tourist Board and consultants put together a bid for funds to the English Tourist Board and Countryside Commission.

The project's aim was 'to improve the visitor management of the area and to promote sustainable tourism'.

The following eight objectives were identified:
- Developing an integrated approach to visitor management.
- Identifying areas which have spare capacity.
- Enhancing the visitors' experience and understanding.
- Promoting environmentally friendly forms of transport.
- Demonstrating the positive links between tourism and the environment.
- Promoting green tourism.
- Involving the local community in implementation.
- Increasing the stock of low cost accommodation.

Organisation and funding

A steering group was established consisting of representatives from the three core funding agencies, Surrey County Council, South East England Tourist Board and Countryside Commission, plus the National Trust and Network South East (later replaced by Thames Trains). Other organisations were co-opted as needed, including three of the District Councils who have recently taken a wider role. The steering group was kept to a manageable size and meets on a quarterly basis, chaired by a Surrey County Council officer.

Working groups have been established to oversee specific initiatives such as at Reigate Hill and Frensham Ponds and provided an opportunity to involve other interests.

A project manager was appointed, working out of the Leisure and Tourism Unit County Hall which provides secretarial and management support.

Financial summary:		
Average annual core budget (1992–1995)£43,000		
Income:	Surrey County Council	38%
	South East England Tourist Board	38%
	Countryside Commission	24%
Expenditure:	Salaries/admin	52%
	Projects	48%

The core budget was supplemented by £34,000 from the Countryside Commission. In addition the project generated a further £186,000 spend on projects from the National Trust and others which wouldn't otherwise have occurred.

Approach

The project manager drew up a detailed work programme based on the original bid. Her involvement in this was seen to be key. Emphasis was placed on practical action rather than spending time drawing up a complex strategy. The programme is updated annually.

Surrey County Council are also piloting a traffic management project — Strategic Traffic Action in Rural Areas (STAR), with the Countryside Commission. There is inevitably some overlap of interests related to traffic generated by visitors. The project officers collaborate on joint projects to pool resources and skills.

The project has concentrated on working with other agencies and local authorities to achieve its ends, rather than getting involved directly with community groups and local organisations. It was felt that communication at this level was best done by the local authorities.

Initiatives undertaken

Encouraging access by public transport

Effort has concentrated on promoting recreational use of the North Downs Line which runs through the heart of the area. With the train operating company and the County Council's Passenger Transport Group, initiatives include a new Sunday service for the intermediate stations, information boards at stations, production and distribution of a poster and leaflet *The North Downs line* and the introduction of free travel on Sundays for holders of the Sunday Rider ticket (see box on page 30). The leaflet has subsequently been incorporated into the Memory Lanes of Surrey leaflet to benefit from a longer print run.

A summer Sunday leisure bus service has been introduced using vintage vehicles. The service has expanded in popularity year by year and is now funded by the County Council's Passenger Transport Group. The service has been promoted via a leaflet *Memory Lanes of Surrey*, 80,000 copies being distributed via libraries, travel centres, information centres and attractions. Sunday Rider tickets giving unlimited travel on buses in Surrey, West Sussex and Hampshire are valid on these routes.

Encouraging walking and cycling

The project has promoted both walking and cycling opportunities. Leaflets have been produced encouraging people to explore the countryside at Box Hill and West Horsley and another leaflet promotes eight easy access trails suitable for wheel chairs and pushchairs. Further leaflets have been produced in conjunction with the National Trust. A leaflet listing all the opportunities for walking in the county entitled *Walking in Surrey* has also been produced and a cycling strategy is currently in preparation.

The Sunday leisure bus service uses old vehicles to attract interest. © Surrey Hills Visitor Project.

Managing sensitive sites

Some key sites needed attention to address problems caused by visitor pressure. The project has been very successful in bringing interests together, securing funding and making things happen at these sites.

At Reigate Hill, the project manager set up a working group involving the National Trust, Countryside Commission and district council. The group agreed a plan to improve the site for visitors by upgrading the car park, removing unsightly structures, building a new information centre, cafe and toilets, a picnic area and alterations to the road access. This project is now being implemented (see box on page 19).

Similarly activity took place at Frensham Common, a popular and intensively used site. A working group established by the project manager, involved the district council and the National Trust. A management plan was prepared including changes to car parking and access, the provision of better interpretation, and zoning for different uses. The project has been instrumental in stimulating action here.

Other initiatives include working with the National Trust at Box Hill to improve interpretation, and at Newlands Corner to create a picnic area, play equipment and interpretation.

Developing under-used assets

The county council owned Norbury Park, was identified as having capacity for more visitors. A working group devised proposals including upgrading the sawmill and workshop as a low key visitor attraction, interpretation of the work of the estate, and an arts project. This is a sensitive area where local people have concerns about encouraging visitors.

The project manager has also spent some time advising Guildford and Godalming Friends of the Earth on their proposals for a camping barn and environmental centre in Puttenham.

Enriching the visitors' experience and understanding

A visitor welcome audit, designed with the Countryside Commission, has been used at all county council sites to identify improvements. This is being used by other site managers in the area.

The project has received much press and media coverage using this to publicise the aims of the project to a wider audience.

The future

The project has been extended for two years with the district councils playing a stronger role and contributing towards core funding.

Assessment

This project has only been up and running for two years but it has already made an impact. It has moved visitor management up the agenda in Surrey, stimulated closer working between local authorities and the agencies in this area, and has demonstrated that action is possible by implementing a number of practical initiatives on the ground, particularly site management and public transport. As a measure of its success the project has been extended with district councils' support. The project has generated interest in securing the appointment of an AONB officer to pursue the wider aims of this designation.

Relatively little effort has been directed towards involving the local community or expanding the stock of accommodation, perhaps eight objectives were over ambitious. Lack of monitoring of many of the initiatives is a known deficiency which needs to be tackled.

Particular achievements

- Action to improve visitor management at key sites. The project has been a catalyst, bringing people together, agreeing a course of action and securing funding. It is acknowledged these improvements would not have taken place without the intervention of the project.
- Public transport. The project has initiated two key projects, the North Downs line and the leisure buses, working closely with appropriate agencies to develop these. Both seem set to continue.
- Stimulating funding. Good use has been made of project funds to lever and stimulate funding from other organisations resulting in visitor management having a higher priority.
- Getting people to work together. The project has improved and revitalised relationships between agencies and local authorities. This is an important and lasting legacy.

Some lessons and pointers

- A project like this can be a powerful catalyst for making things happen. Key features are a project manager who commands respect, independence from the existing agencies and funding to pump prime initiatives.

The Wiltshire Downs Project — The art of access

A project combining public access and community arts events to generate interest in sustainable tourism.

Location:	Wiltshire.
Partners:	Countryside Commission, West Country Tourist Board, Southern Arts, British Waterways, Wiltshire County Council, Kennet District Council.
Structure:	Advisory Steering Group and full time project officer.
Timescale:	June 1993 – June 1996
Core funding:	£46,000 annual average (including £10,000 support in kind)

Points of interest:
- Riding, cycling and walking routes.
- Partnership with Southern Arts, arts events and initiatives.
- imaginative marketing.

Context

The project area, 500 sq km of east Wiltshire within the North Wessex Downs Area of Outstanding Natural Beauty, is a mixture of attractive open chalk downland and lower lying farmland. It is of great archaeological importance and includes Avebury World Heritage Site, the main reason why people visit the area. The area, which mostly falls within the district of Kennet, has a low tourism profile and the few small tourism enterprises there wish to see more visitors.

Origins and objectives

The Wiltshire Downs Project was the idea of the Countryside Commission who wished to see improved interpretation of the historic downs landscape, linked with recreation. This coincided with the West Country Tourist Board and the local authorities establishing a comprehensive tourism development action programme throughout the county, the Wiltshire Tourism Project.

The aim of the Wiltshire Downs Project is to promote tourism which ensures that the environment and the quality of life of those who live and work in the area is enhanced and the economic wellbeing of the area improved.

Consultants prepared a strategy and action programme for the Wiltshire Downs area which became the framework for the project.

The objectives were:
- ensuring tourism development is based on the area's intrinsic character, supporting their conservation and enjoyment;
- raising the profile of those places which can absorb visitors – thereby deflecting pressure from Avebury;
- managing visitor pressures around Avebury;
- raising the contribution tourism makes to the economy, including farm diversification;
- convincing the commercial sector of the long term benefits to them of this approach, so stimulating private investment and political and practical support for conservation;
- measuring the effectiveness of this approach and gauging the applicability of the ideas elsewhere in Wiltshire.

Organisation and funding

Originally the Downs project was run by a project officer employed by the Tourism project. Following formal termination of the Tourism project, the officer moved to the Kennet District Council offices. The original co-location and relationship between the Downs project and Tourism project did not work smoothly, with confusion between roles and occasional competition for funding.

A steering group is chaired by the Countryside Commission and includes Kennet District Council and Southern Arts as funding agencies. Previously, Wiltshire County Council, Tourism project and the West Country Tourist Board were also involved.

An advisory group of 20 organisations meets twice yearly, consisting of conservation or land management interests. Although having limited influence it has been useful for liaison and making contacts.

The project, initially planned for two years, has been extended for a third year because of the progress made.

Financial summary:		
Average annual core budget: £46,000		
Income:	Countryside Commission	50%
	Kennet District Council	12.5%
	Southern Arts	12.5%
	Wiltshire Tourism Project/ Kennet District Council in kind	25%
Expenditure:	Salaries and admin	70%
	Projects	30%

Additional money has been raised to fund particular initiatives.

Approach

The project officer found the strategy a useful guide, but as it was written without resource limits, in practice expectations had to be tailored to fit the available budget. Additional ad hoc opportunities have also been pursued if related to the strategy's aims.

Occasionally objectives identified were pursued outside the project, for example, a visitor management initiative in Avebury started before the project was established. Some marketing activities were carried out by the Tourism project or the tourism unit at Kennet District Council. Some public transport proposals were pursued by Wiltshire County Council. Given its limited resources, the project concentrated on smaller tangible activities, including route identification, information provision, interpretation and events.

Initiatives undertaken

Community arts activity

A strong feature has been the use of the arts in countryside information and interpretation, making use of local artistic talent.

In 1994 the Cherhill Down Ramble, a participatory theatrical event held over four evenings, was developed with and enacted by the local community in the village of Cherhill. This imaginative event involved re-chalking the Cherhill White Horse met a number of the project's objectives at once (see box on page 41).

The project plans to set up more community arts events, hoping to involve local businesses partly to involve and interest them in future sponsorship.

The project used a local artist to create a striking events poster publicising countryside, community and arts events provided by local organisations. Southern Arts are supporting a separate full colour 'guide to arts and crafts' based on a similar brochure in Hampshire and Dorset.

Working with the Public Arts Officer in Thamesdown an arts-related scheme is being planned for the Chiseldon – Marlborough Railway Path, linking the Great Western Community Forest with the Downs and Savernake Forest, involving an artist in residence.

Cycling, riding and walking routes

Leaflets have been published on cycling and riding routes in the area. Cycle routes were researched by the project officer and riding routes by the British Horse Society. Volunteer help with the cycling routes proved inaccurate; the exercise had to be repeated. Checking the detailed routes and the print was very demanding, more time was needed.

Imaginative use of art in countryside information material. © *Wiltshire Downs Project.*

The leaflets have proved very popular, the original print run was 5,000 and a second edition has been fully taken up. Distribution outside the project area has proved difficult. Lack of funding for a targeted marketing campaign was a weakness. Advertising in the British Tourist Authority brochure brought little response but a press feature in the Cyclist Touring Club magazine was successful. Enterprises on the routes have mailed the material to enquirers. Riding stables near the riding route reported little impact on enquiries during the first summer season following publication, better monitoring will take place during 1995.

The Project has supported the development of walking routes working successfully with Pewsey village. This has resulted in a new footpath link creating a circular route. A canal walk round Pewsey was also prepared for British Waterways. A series of eight circular walks leaflets prepared by the County Council has also proved popular, although they were not themed as originally proposed, highlighting the need for strict guidelines if work is to be carried out by others.

Training and enterprise liaison

Training for small rural businesses was identified as a need in the strategy. Together with Wiltshire Training and Enterprise Council and Kennet District Council, the Project established marketing and management courses. Promotion was by mail and phone, but attendance was very low (four on the business course). Feedback showed many local businesses were only part time and not interested in improving their skills or knowledge.

Kennet District Council is now seeking to produce a local tourist business newsletter, to get enterprises more aware of each other, to put over green ideas to them and to lay the groundwork for a tourist association.

Orientating the visitor

A full colour leaflet and cartoon-based map was produced for the 1995 season to orientate the visitor and promote the special character of the area. It also aids visitor management by encouraging visitors to leave their cars in the surrounding 'gateway' market towns. It will be important to assess how useful the leaflet has been.

The future

Future proposals include creating a long distance circular walk and riding route, a local produce report, further arts events and attracting sponsorship from local firms.

An exit strategy is now being developed, probably leading to integration with the mainstream tourism and environmental work of Kennet District Council and with the management of the North Wessex Downs Area of Outstanding Natural Beauty.

Assessment

Valuable work has been achieved in encouraging agencies and enterprises to work together. The initial strategy was clearly too ambitious given the project's resources. It has sensibly concentrated on small scale practical initiatives with tangible success for instance at Pewsey and through the creative Cherhill Down Ramble.

Monitoring has been limited, due to limited resources, and much of the publicity has not been available long enough to assess effect. Marketing resources port for the project have been weak, diminishing the potential for the countryside access and interpretation material to have much influence on incoming visitors. Impact on deflecting visitor pressure from Avebury or influencing car use are likely to have been slight.

The Wiltshire Tourism Project should have been in a position to provide the necessary marketing context for the project. However, timing was wrong for this and the relationship between the two projects was not always constructive.

Particular achievements

- Changing local perceptions. The District and County Councils are now more alert to the value of sustainable tourism to the local economy and community. Local people and conservation groups have also responded well, seeing how tourism and conservation can work together.
- Demonstrating a relationship between the arts and rural tourism. A particular success. The involvement of Southern Arts provided a fresh, creative force. The Cherhill event had many benefits showing how diverse local organisations and age groups could work together. It has also alerted Southern Arts, the Countryside Commission and other agencies of the wider connections between arts, countryside recreation and tourism.
- Providing an approach and an infrastructure which can be built upon. The area previously lacked effective information material on routes for countryside recreation and events. The Project has begun to provide this and shown how it can be integrated with tourism.

Some lessons and pointers

- Ensure related projects are fully supportive. Better integration between the Tourism project and Downs project would have helped.
- Make sure that initial strategies and action programmes reflect the resources available for implementation, or set out alternative options.
- Allow time to develop routes and associated print, as the attention to detail required is time consuming. Don't rely on others to do the work unless you are sure of their ability.
- When planning print and seeking funds for it, make sure that its distribution and promotion is identified and properly costed at the outset.
- Don't dabble in training schemes. Successful training requires considerable resources to identify local needs and tailor programmes and delivery.
- Arts in the countryside has great creative potential to raise the profile of an area, attracting visitors and involving local people. Local artists can articulate what local people feel about an area.

The Tarka Project — Green with a theme

A project which uses the theme of Tarka the Otter to promote sustainable tourism and conservation within the same project, based on conservation initiatives, sustainable tourism products, information and marketing.

Location:	North Devon
Partners:	Countryside Commission, Rural Development Commission, West Country Tourist Board, Devon County Council, Mid Devon District Council, North Devon District Council, Torridge District Council, West Devon Borough Council.
Structure:	Project steering group. Small executive team, some externally funded.
Timescale:	1989–1997
Core funding:	£90,000 annual average.

Points of interest:
- Embracing both tourism and conservation work.
- Relationship with private sector — establishing a tourism association.
- Walking and cycling route development and marketing.
- How the work and priorities have changed over time.

Context

This project is based in the area of north Devon which formed the setting for the classic novel *Tarka the Otter* written by Henry Williamson in the 1920s. It is a varied area, with traditional holiday destinations on the coast and relatively remote inland areas which receive few visitors and seek economic diversification. It is rich in conservation value. Maintaining habitats and improving water quality is important in conserving the otter population as well as other wildlife.

Origins and objectives

The concept of the project came from conservation interests within Devon County Council. A primary motive was to encourage more resources to be spent on conservation, by demonstrating its value for tourism — ie through the project an economic argument for conservation could be made. At the same time, a genuine need to strengthen the economic benefit to communities through tourism was recognised.

Compared with Devon's National Parks and Heritage Coasts, it was felt that the area had no identity to act as a catalyst for either conservation and tourism initiatives. Tarka the Otter was lighted upon as a theme to rectify this.

The aims set out in a strategy document of 1988 were, and remain:
- to protect and enrich the wildlife, natural beauty and character of the area;
- to encourage public enjoyment, appreciation and understanding of the area;
- to promote tourism and recreation;
- to demonstrate that conservation can make a significant contribution to the social and economic wellbeing of the area.

A guiding principle has been the welfare of the otter population and other wildlife communities, with no disturbance to habitats in areas promoted by the project.

Organisation and funding

The project is overseen by a Project Group, made up of officers from the county council, four district councils and the Countryside Commission.

There is no direct member-level involvement by the local authorities, which may have been a disadvantage in securing political commitment.

Strong branding, making full use of the Tarka theme. ©Tarka Project.

The tourism industry is not represented directly, though contact with them is maintained by the Tourist Association (see below).

Staffing has been quite flexible, with some posts coopted or separately funded. The initial Otter Conservation Officer, for example, was funded through commercial sponsorship from Intervet and South West Water. The current project team includes:

- a full time project officer;
- a part time administrator;
- a recently appointed interpretation officer, employed through the European Union LIFE Programme;
- a conservation officer, as a shared post with Devon Wildlife Trust;
- an access officer, as a permanent member of the County Council countryside team, responsible for the Tarka Trail, the Two Moors Way and other access work.

The project was originally conceived as lasting three years but has been significantly extended, reflecting strong local support from a consultation exercise.

Financial summary:

Annual average core budget (1993–1995): £90,000

Income (first six years):

Devon County Council		50%
Countryside Commission		33%
Local Authorities		17%

Expenditure:	Salaries and admin.	62%
	Projects	38%

Approach

There have been three phases to the project. The first years concentrated on conservation work and the creation of the Tarka Trail. The next phase concentrated on winning support from the industry through the establishment of the Tarka Country Tourist Association. The most recent phase has placed more emphasis on communicating with visitors, through customer care and interpretation. Over time there has been increasing emphasis on supporting the local economy through tourism, and a recognition of the need for marketing.

Until recently there has been relatively little monitoring. On reflection an initial survey of visitors would have been helpful, as a baseline.

Initiatives

Conservation work

A conservation officer has been part of the team for most of the Project's life. Advice has been given to landowners on conservation issues. Sites and habitats needing management have received attention and emphasis has been placed on otter conservation work. Locations promoted by the project have been monitored for any damage suffered, which has been minimal.

The link with tourism has given weight to the Project's conservation work and authority to its views. For example, strong representation on water quality issues made by the Project have been strengthened by its position as a tourism project with economic relevance.

Conservation work has culminated in the preparation of a Rivers and Wetland Strategy and programme, in a unique partnership with various agencies.

Communication and networking

Local awareness of the Project and the Tarka theme has been high, and a great deal of media support has been received. A number of local firms and organisations have taken up the Tarka name and a regular project newsletter is produced.

An important reflection of the Tarka theme has been the adoption of the name by a separate project formed to promote the Exeter to Barnstaple line (the Tarka Line) — promotional leaflets, walks, educational packs and panels in stations have been produced.

Take up of the concept by tourism businesses was slower than initially envisaged. However, this was strengthened by the formation of the Tarka Country Tourist Association, as a network of enterprises which embrace the principles of sustainable tourism advocated through the project (see box on page 44). Membership has grown steadily to 150, and the Association has become responsible for various marketing activities with support from the Project team.

A 'Producers Group' has been formed of around 20 enterprises producing local crafts and foods. The group was established as part of the Tourist Association, creating a natural mechanism for producers to promote their wares to other members. A map based promotional leaflet has been produced and a distribution service and a retail outlet established by members.

The Association decided to set up a 'Friends of Tarka' scheme to invite visitors to make a donation to support local conservation and to go onto a mailing list, with 100 people joining in 18 months. Association members are pursuing ways of raising funds for conservation.

Marketing

Marketing was initially undertaken by the Project but is now mainly the responsibility of the Association. Publicity has involved:

- A small advertising campaign. This appears to have had limited impact, due to lack of budget.
- Journalists visits and articles. These were more successful. National TV and newspaper coverage generated a lot of response.
- Exposure in existing local authority destination brochures. This has been important in generating response. However, some local authorities might have made more of the Tarka theme and given it greater coverage in their print.
- A special West Country Tourist Board leaflet about Tarka Country, distributed through the normal channels and used to answer enquiries. The effect of this is not known, but although useful it lacked strong images or messages.
- Coverage in the Celebrate the Countryside campaign which seems to have generated very few enquiries.

Much of the advertising and media work was initially aimed at niche markets, eg through the walking press. On reflection this was too restrictive; the main market is for people who want a rural/coastal holiday or break and wish to dabble in 'green' activities such as walking or cycling.

The Association has received around 750 enquiries in the last year, a significant proportion coming from exposure in local authority guides. Conversion rates have not been measured.

The Association decided to produce its own guide to Tarka Country, using an A5 sized report with sensitive area descriptions, green themes, listing and adverts from members. Distribution has proved costly and time consuming, yet Association members are supportive of the guide and have doubled their advertising spend in it.

A requirement of Association membership is to provide guests with information and an understanding of Tarka Country. An information distribution service for members has been established through an appointed sales agent, and a distinctive Tarka literature rack has been produced out of hazel whips.

The Tarka Trail and other routes

The Tarka Trail is an 180 mile long distance walking route. It is a figure of eight, including a link which involves taking the Tarka Line train. Part of the trail is on the South West Coast Path, a well used national trail.

The trail has helped to bring all parts of the project area together and create a focus. It took a lot of effort to set up, yet some problems are still being ironed out. Route planning was quite rushed to meet the timetable, and it could have been made more interesting with less lane walking and more linking to villages and points of interest. It was planned for the long distance walker, yet the terrain is more appealing to people seeking a short walks — a bigger market.

Two organisations, including Devon Wildlife Trust are offering walking holiday packages on the trail, but individual accommodation enterprises do not appear to be making the most of it. Promotion has been through a saleable trail guide and special interest media as part of the overall marketing of the area. Recent surveys found that 11 per cent of users had been attracted to the trail by coverage in the media.

More recently effort has concentrated on promoting shorter circular walks, sometimes in partnership with village communities such as Hatherleigh and Great Torrington. Comprehensive 'Where to walk' leaflets have been prepared and a similar leaflet produced for cycling.

A 30 mile stretch of the Tarka Trail, round the estuaries, is also a cycle trail, which was developed in a related initiative by the County Council. This has proved extremely popular, with about 75,000 cyclists present over the four month summer period. Ten cycle hire enterprises have recently been formed along the route. No physical problems of overuse have emerged, but there is some conflict with walkers. The route is being extended both north and south.

Interpretation

Interpretation work has been fairly limited. Currently visitors receive a fragmented picture. A new approach has been to develop a joint comprehensive interpretation strategy, in consultation with other interpretation providers in the area. A number of themes and messages have been identified.

Rather than seeking one central visitor centre to interpret Tarka Country the approach has been to create a number of sites which interlink, thereby helping to spread visitor use across the area. Six centres have been established already.

In 1994 the project produced a compendium report of events, having previously laid on their own events and guided walks. A number of local interpretative initiatives have been pursued with rural communities.

The future

The Project has core funding until 1997. The Association is seen as playing an increasingly important role, enabling the objectives of the project to be properly integrated within the local tourism industry. Funding has been sought for a development officer to be attached to the Association. Membership targets have been set at 240 over the next three years, and a programme of action has been identified.

The interpretation strategy has deliberately been prepared in conjunction with other organisations, so it has a life beyond the project. Ongoing maintenance of the Tarka Trail will be the responsibility of the County Council.

Conservation objectives will be met through the ongoing commitment of partnership organisations to the Strategy for Rivers and Wetlands, with funding supported by a tourism heritage trust involving the Association.

Assessment

This has been a sizeable, creative project which has achieved a considerable profile, already providing ideas for others to follow. The logical development of the project from infrastructure work, to enterprise liaison and then interpretation to the visitor, provides a useful model. The juxtaposition of tourism and conservation work within the same project has given both aspects credibility.

The relationship with the private sector has been encouraging. Local authorities have recognised the value of the project in broadening the image and opportunities of the area away from the coast, but more needs to be done to integrate it with their mainstream tourism marketing.

The overall impact on visitor numbers and their behaviour is perhaps not as clear as one might have hoped after five years. Response to marketing has been positive but limited.

Particular achievements

- Changing attitudes. Creating a greater appreciation of the link between tourism and conservation, gaining economic credibility for an environmental approach. Maintaining environmental principles at the core of all the project's work.
- Awareness and take up of the Tarka theme. The project has provided the area with an identity.
- The establishment and growth of the Tourist Association. Leaving behind a strong Association which has a varied membership and is actively promoting green principles.
- The development of the Tarka Trail as a tangible physical legacy, which can be amended and built upon where necessary. The opportunities provided for both cycling and walking and links with the railway line is a strength.

Some lessons and pointers

- Try to secure involvement from those responsible for tourism marketing from the start. As a conservation led project, tourism officers did not have initial commitment to it.
- Know your market before developing tourism products. The Trail might have been planned rather differently if it had been based on a closer assessment of the kinds of walkers who might be attracted to this area.
- Do not underestimate the time, cost and ongoing maintenance associated with developing trails.
- Establish the right mechanisms for the private sector to respond to sustainable tourism concepts and to work together to develop them. The Association shows what can be achieved with this.

The North Pennines Tourism Partnership — England's last wilderness

A project to develop and market rural tourism in a remote upland area, based on and maintaining its intrinsic qualities.

Location:	In and surrounding the North Pennines Area of Outstanding Natural Beauty on the borders of Cumbria, Northumberland and Durham.
Partners:	Countryside Commission, English Tourist Board, Rural Development Commission, Cumbria Tourist Board, Northumbria Tourist Board, Cumbria County Council, Durham County Council, Northumberland County Council, Eden District Council, Teesdale District Council, Tynedale District Council, Wear Valley District Council, Parish Councils, North Pennines Heritage Trust, National Farmers Union.
Structure:	Committee of partners, management group and various working groups. Full time project manager and secretary.
Timescale:	1990–1996. Ongoing funding being sought.
Core funding:	£41,000 annual average

Points of interest:
- Sound communication and confidence building.
- Parallel training initiative.
- Creating an identity for an area.
- Destination and short breaks marketing.

Context

The North Pennines is a remote, bleak yet beautiful high moorland area, bisected by the upper reaches of Tyne, Tees and Wear valleys. It is the most sparsely populated area of its size in England and contains many important nature reserves and conservation areas. In 1988 it was designated as an Area of Outstanding Natural Beauty. Tourism is a potentially valuable source of income for the remote rural communities, and already contributes to one third of the jobs in the area. The area, unified by its landscape, falls within six separate districts and three counties and has tended to be treated as marginal to each of them.

Origins and objectives

Attempts over the last twenty years to coordinate tourism were only partially successful, lacking a clear means of implementation. In 1988 a consultant's report recommended a Tourism Development Action Programme. At the same time designation as an Area of Outstanding Natural Beauty was announced, amid local fears that it would fossilise the area and exacerbate economic problems.

To address this local concern the English Tourist Board, Rural Development Commission and Countryside Commission agreed jointly to support a rural Tourism Development Action Programme. Public meetings were held to promote this, recognising that local involvement was crucial.

The Partnership objectives are concerned with strengthening rural tourism:
- improving image and marketing;
- improving quality and standards at existing attractions and accommodation;
- seeking modest development appropriate to the environment;
- improving business advice and training;
- promoting informal countryside activities;
- developing rural arts and crafts; and
- conserving the character and appearance of the landscape, towns and villages.

A key aim of the agencies was to show that economic development through tourism can be compatible with landscape designation. The Partnership has therefore followed the guiding principles of the Government Task Force, linking the visitor, place and host community.

Organisation and funding

The Partnership has a Manager and part time secretary/assistant. Supervision has been through the Cumbria Tourist Board who acted as treasurer. There is a Management Group of officers from the national agencies.

A Partnership Committee meets twice a year to oversee the project. It includes councillors from the seven local authorities, representatives of the national agencies, the National Farmers' Union, and the North Pennines Heritage Trust, a voluntary conservation society, plus representatives of the private sector and parish councils. This works effectively as a well balanced forum.

Work is devolved through two working groups covering development and marketing, and separate topic groups have also been formed. This structure is good for involving lots of people, but is rather unwieldy with much of the implementation falling to the Partnership Manager.

Hartside viewpoint — effective interpretation at key locations.
© Richard Denman.

Financial Summary (1994–1995):

Annual average core income:		£41,000
Income:	Rural Development	
	Commission	20%
	Countryside Commission	28%
	County Councils	33%
	District Councils	19%
Additional project income:		£19,000
Expenditure:	Salaries and administration	54%
	Projects	56%

A separate 'North Pennines Business and Training Initiative' was established as a parallel three year project from the same office. It is able to tap new sources of funding from training bodies. Average annual core funding has been approximately £35,000.

Approach

The approach is to work with the local communities and businesses. The central office in Alston aids good communication as people tend to drop in. A regular newsletter is effective in raising profile. The success of this was shown by a survey of local businesses which found that 60 per cent had been in contact with the Partnership. There was strong support for its activities, with an appreciation amongst tourism enterprises about the need to conserve the natural heritage.

The consultants' report and a marketing plan provide the context, but most of the practical initiatives have come from the working groups.

Initial emphasis was on image building, marketing and training and advisory work, to create awareness and confidence, especially amongst tourism enterprises. More recently the Partnership has been pursuing interpretation work and raising funds for conservation.

Market research amongst visitors in 1990 and 1991 helped guide the Partnership's activities. Further surveys are planned for 1995. Individual activities have also been monitored.

Initiatives undertaken

Marketing

A key approach has been to get others to promote the special identity of the area through their own marketing. A very simple, crisp logo was developed using strong green and purple colours, together with the slogan 'England's last wilderness'. This has been well used. For example, owing to the awareness generated, a commercial publisher has produced a good quality visitor newspaper *The North Pennines Messenger* in association with the Partnership but at no cost to them.

Print and promotion has been kept simple, partly due to low budgets and the need not to duplicate the existing marketing of local authorities or tourist boards. Local tourism enterprises are too small to support new glossy print. A small free colour flyer has been produced for everyone in the area to use in mailings to generate awareness and a single colour accommodation list is used to service enquiries. A saleable map was produced which served to identify the area and orientate visitors but has proved hard to distribute. An initial destination advertising campaign in the Radio Times was dropped owing to poor response. Emphasis has been switched to press work, distribution, direct mail and working through tourism officers. There has been no specific monitoring of this marketing.

A recent focus has been themed short break campaigns. The first of these, 'Blustery Breaks', generated £100,000 worth of media coverage, which was the main purpose of the promotion, though visitor numbers were limited (see box on page 23).

Countryside activities and attractions

Outdoor activity centres have been brought together and links created between them and local authority countryside staff. The latter have worked with accommodation operators to develop local walks. Advice has been given to local attractions, including encouraging longer opening hours. A feasibility study was supported on a focal visitor centre for the area in the old town hall, Alston.

Arts and Crafts

Craft enterprises have been assisted with marketing through coordination of exhibition work and the creation of the 'North Pennines Produce Trail' promoted by a leaflet. Monitoring showed good take up of the leaflet, with the majority of craft outlets recording more visitors and 25 per cent increased sales.

Infrastructure and conservation work

Work with local people to prepare an interpretation strategy for the area is been reflected in the AONB Management Plan. Interpretation on the ground will be taken forward through specific community groups. A study on strategic tourist information points, in shops, pubs etc is ready for implementation when funds are available. An initial infrastructure survey has led to small improvements to car parking etc.

A North Pennines Green Tourism Award Scheme was created to raise environmental awareness amongst the tourism industry, and enterprises were invited to come up with their own 'ideas for greening'. A pilot project to raise money for conservation is currently being pursued. This will include using specially designed collecting boxes and 'free' bookmarks in tourism outlets to encourage visitors to donate money in support of conservation projects in the North Pennines.

Work has been undertaken to coordinate and promote public transport services, primarily through the high quality leaflet *Across the Roof of England* (see box on page 27).

Business advice and training

Initially on its own and more recently through the Business and Training Initiative, the project has handled over 700 business enquiries and 175 in depth advisory sessions and contributed to 82 training events. Response has been good. A key to success has been the central office and the ability to deliver advice and training very locally, often on site. One third of enquiries have come from would-be operators, the rest from existing enterprises. Most topics relate to marketing and business advice, and environmental issues have also been covered.

One third of all the current tourism businesses in the area started trading during the lifetime of the project.

The future

The Partnership was set up in 1990 for three years. Partners all agreed it should continue and funding is secured until 1996 with agreement in principle for support to 1998 from some local authorities.

The Partnership's approach is increasingly reflected by the local authorities, who are more frequently featuring the North Pennines in their work. Recently the Partnership helped a North Pennines Tourism Association to form, with 42 members. It is strongly committed to conservation principles and will help to implement some projects in the future. The Partnership has made a valued contribution to the AONB Management Plan.

Assessment

Based on principles of sustainability, the Partnership has very successfully performed a rural tourism marketing, development and training role in an area previously lacking in focus owing to isolation and location on the fringes of a number of authorities. Concentrating initially on building awareness, making itself relevant to tourism enterprises and gaining their confidence, has been a sound approach, creating a secure basis for building conservation and interpretation work.

Although monitoring has been undertaken, it has been hard to identify the amount of new tourism actually generated through the Partnership. Possibly, the project has tried to do too much with too little resources and in some cases individual partners might have been persuaded to take the lead themselves rather than relying on the manager. A greater involvement in development projects might leave a more tangible long term benefit in the community.

Particular achievements

- Excellent communication with small local businesses and communities. There is a positive atmosphere in the area towards tourism and strong support for the project. Working in parallel with a training and advisory service has been valuable.
- Genuine partnership. Use of the word 'partnership' has proved appropriate. A good balance has been achieved and the structure has meant that many organisations and individuals have become involved.
- Greater acceptance of the relationship between tourism and the environment. The embracing of conservation principles by the private sector has flowed from the Partnership's work. It also influenced the new AONB Management Plan, properly reflecting the role of tourism.
- Generating awareness. The logo and slogan have been effectively taken up. With limited resources good promotion has been achieved on the back of others. Extensive media coverage was generated through Blustery Breaks.

Some lessons and pointers

- A central office, accessible to all, and independent of any local authority or agency office, is a great strength.
- Creating large working groups can be good for local democracy but is time consuming and may discourage organisations from taking on the work themselves.
- Training and advice needs to be locally based. The uptake of this has been better than in many other rural areas, with local delivery often the reason.
- Separate small scale marketing schemes can generate good publicity but often low volumes.
- A lot can be achieved simply by getting people to communicate better and building on existing initiatives.

South Somerset District Council — Sharing the secret

This is not a discrete project but an example of a District Council with an active and sensitive approach to developing rural tourism and public access combined with a professional marketing campaign.

Location:	South Somerset
Partners:	Countryside Commission, South Somerset District Council.
Structure:	District Council Tourism Unit, working with Countryside Unit.
Timescale:	Approach followed from late 1980s.
Core funding:	£184,000 annual marketing budget.

Points of interest:
- Integration between tourism and countryside management.
- Adoption of sustainable tourism approach in mainstream tourism work.
- Successful promotion of walking trails, with attention to detail.
- General rural tourism marketing.
- Monitoring recognised as important to secure support.
- Strong member level involvement.

Context

South Somerset is a large rural district of attractive, rolling countryside, mainly farmland and scattered woodland with pleasant villages and market towns. It has no coast, national parks or nationally well known landscape or heritage features, yet it is appealing to visitors largely through its traditional and well conserved rural atmosphere. The tourism industry consists of small scale accommodation and heritage attractions. There are no obvious problems from visitor pressure, though communities are cautious about attracting too many visitors, fearing that may destroy the appeal of the area for all. South Somerset is typical of rural England away from the coasts, national parks and urban centres.

Origins and objectives

The Council's involvement in tourism began in 1985, when it decided, for economic reasons, to try to increase its share of tourism to Somerset, most of which was going to Exmoor and the coast. A Tourism Panel of councillors was formed with a broad spectrum of opinion about tourism.

Policy emerged to create 'a selective and sensitive form of tourism which helped the local economy and respected conservation'.

A Tourism Strategy was prepared setting out a comprehensive range of marketing activities and development functions. In parallel with this, the District Council accepted responsibility for public rights of way from the County Council. The tourism potential of rights of way was quickly identified. Expenditure on them was doubled and a footpaths officer appointed, developing later into a full countryside unit with a strong tourism justification.

Organisation and funding

A Tourism Officer and assistant have responsibility for implementing the tourism policy, as well as corporate marketing and PR The Tourism Panel of council members proved critical in enabling strong and consistent support for tourism work.

Initially, the countryside unit was integrated with tourism within a Leisure and Arts department. This was particularly important in ensuring that countryside work was undertaken in a tourism context and vice versa.

There is no formal involvement of the private sector or local communities in the Council's work. It was felt that the District was too big and enterprises too disparate for a single tourist association. Instead consultation is through four tourism workshops held regularly across the district exchanging ideas and fostering links. The Council has also supported networks of enterprises in their own marketing — eg garden attractions.

Financial summary:	
Total annual tourism budget:	£184,000
Salaries and admin (including tourist information centres)	46%
Marketing and research	54%

A number of countryside infrastructure and marketing initiatives received Countryside Commission support as well as a district-wide countryside management service.

Approach

The Council pursued sensitive promotion of rural tourism before the concept of 'sustainability' became current. Building tourism on the intrinsic qualities of the countryside and making the most of walking and cycling were seen as a logical approach anyway, attracting visitors who care about the environment, rather than trying to change visitors' attitudes. This is seen as a large market.

The approach is largely marketing led. Market research on visitors to Somerset showed the importance of countryside images and access. Specific walking, cycling and short break products were established on this basis, all professionally promoted, and fine tuned according to feedback from visitors. Regular monitoring has been essential in securing member level commitment during this economically stringent period.

The portfolio of print has been extremely well designed and well integrated, with a corporate identity 'Share the Secret', portraying an upmarket image and a feeling of privileged discovery.

Initiatives

Walking and cycling promotion

Work on rights of way has been largely stimulated and led by tourism considerations. An early product was a carefully researched set of ten walks, waymarked on the ground and described on high quality laminated cards within a sealable pack. Packs were distributed to retail and information outlets and were subject to a separate tourism marketing campaign, with advertising in specialist media such as Country Walking and associated PR work. 800 enquiries were generated from a trial advertising campaign in 1987, a good result for saleable print. Feedback cards were inserted in each pack generating a sizeable response and many favourable comments. Armed with this evidence the approach was continued, and a further three sets of walks researched, waymarked and promoted. Between 1987 and 1994, 34,000 walks packs were sold.

Promoting trails to walkers is a strong component of tourism in South Somerset. © South Somerset DC.

The circular walks, of which there are now 40 in total, are quite short (up to two hours) to meet market needs. They also serve an economic development purpose, being well distributed through the district and particularly orientated to less visited villages.

Comprehensive monitoring of all the Council's services found that the circular walks were the most recognised and applauded of all their activities, used by 27 per cent of residents.

The Leland and Liberty trails, two regional walking routes based on historical themes have been developed. They were carefully planned to meet market requirements and to bring spending to less visited communities. They have created a specific tourism product in keeping with the environment, and have been well promoted and monitored (see box on page 19).

An on-road cycle route has been promoted. 70,000 leaflets have been distributed, with many enquiries generated from the District's own short breaks guide. Individual enterprises on the route report good business. Off-road cycling routes are now being developed.

Country breaks and wider marketing

The main marketing of South Somerset is through a full colour, A4 sized brochure, *Country Breaks*, rich with rural images. The approach is to sell the image, but to keep the product flexible and relevant to a wide market. The brochure contains only a few packages or specific break offers and mainly provides information on accommodation and attractions. Standardised illustrated entries are used and costs of entry are low to encourage participation by small businesses.

A special Classic Gardens offer has also been developed, with accommodation showing a flower symbol offering discounted admission to a network of gardens. This has generated press interest but only 300 redeemed tickets in the last year.

Monitoring the brochure in 1993 entailed:

- Mailing a questionnaire to 5,000 recipients of the guide. Of 1,200 respondents, 60 per cent had visited the area in the last three years and 27 per cent had made a booking through the brochure.
- Producing a record pad for enterprises to use to record enquiries. 20 accommodation enterprises making regular recordings showed 25 per cent of bookings coming from the brochure or tourist information centres.
- A printed questionnaire in the guide itself. 600 returns provided feedback on visitor profiles and use.

From this it was estimated that Country Breaks brought in £3.5m in spending, persuading the Council to increase the print run from 40,000 to 100,000. Direct mail has been particularly effective and now accounts for half the distribution, derived from previous enquirers and carefully targeted purchased lists. A £10,000 advertising campaign generated 6,000 new enquiries.

Walking and cycling products are seen as very important to tourism marketing and vice versa and are heavily featured in the brochure. A telephone survey of 100 recipients found a majority reporting that the coverage of walking and cycling was critically important in encouraging them to come to the area.

The District has diminished its niche marketing of walking and cycling through specialist media because of the poor cost per response. Rather, they are using these products in more general print and campaigns to attract a wider market.

Pursuing other green themes

The Council has promoted green consciousness through the Country Breaks brochure which included in 1994 a 'green page' with a checklist for visitors on how to be green (take a guided walk, use public transport etc), linked to relevant information in the guide. It also suggested donations to three local environmental projects, although this generated little response. In 1995 the equivalent feature has placed greater emphasis on local products and rural distinctiveness.

The future

The Council is continuing to develop its walking and cycling products and is seeking to attract more external funding. They will continue monitoring and refine their marketing with greater use of direct mail and information technology.

They would like to develop joint marketing with other similar rural areas outside the national parks.

Assessment

This is an example of District Council which has adopted a very professional approach to marketing rural tourism and maintained this consistently for a number of years. Many principles of sustainable tourism have been applied naturally as they make good sense in tourism terms, especially building on the intrinsic appeal of the countryside and walking and cycling opportunities.

Perhaps the Council could have pursued overtly sustainable initiatives such as the promotion of public transport or local produce. However, such initiatives might have deflected them from their main aim of strengthening the rural economy. It will be easier for them to include these elements now they have established credibility and skill in mainstream rural tourism marketing.

Particular achievements

- The very high quality images and design in print, with great attention to detail. This appears to have been fundamental to high response levels.
- A close working relationship between members and officers. The commitment of the Tourism Panel, nurtured through careful feedback, has ensured continued support.
- Developing walking routes into a successful tourism product, as opposed to just a facility that is available. This requires active promotion.

Some lessons and pointers

- Monitoring can help to drive action forward. The Council has used various methods, all have been important in fine tuning their approach.
- Integration of countryside and tourism functions is very helpful. This enabled the Council to take a positive approach towards marketing countryside access.
- Don't rely simply on niche marketing. The Council found this was restricting potential.
- Working just within one District makes things much simpler to organise.
- Focusing on achievable objectives and keeping these up over a sustained period is a good recipe for success.

The Lake District Traffic Management Initiative — Managing the car

A project creating a comprehensive, integrated approach to tackling a range of transport issues across the Lake District National Park, including those relating to tourism.

Location:	The Lake District National Park, Cumbria.
Partners:	Countryside Commission, Cumbria Tourist Board, Lake District National Park Authority, Cumbria County Council.
Structure:	Steering Group, Advisory Panel, system of working and action groups. Two full time project officers.
Timescale:	1993–1996
Core funding:	£40,000 annual average.

Points of interest:
- Comprehensive approach to traffic management.
- Concept of a roads hierarchy.
- Lessons learnt on the need to local consultation.
- Linking public transport to the needs of countryside access.
- Experience and problems with transport information delivery and marketing.

Context

The Lake District is Britain's second most visited national park, receiving 20 million visitor days per year. Tourism provides the mainstay of the local economy. The tourism industry, visitors and local people depend heavily on cars, yet high levels of traffic, unmanaged car parking and periodic congestion are at times intrusive and hazardous, spoiling the opportunity for 'quiet enjoyment' for which the National Park was designated. Local traffic volumes are rising and, if left unchecked, national forecasts of traffic growth suggest that the Lake District will suffer increasingly severe problems.

Origins and objectives

This initiative stemmed from:
- A working group of the County Council Highways Department, the National Park and the Cumbria Tourist Board, which reviewed the traffic situation. They agreed that individually they did not have the time or resources to carry out the necessary research, consultation and action, and recommended a partnership approach with a joint project officer.
- Following a Heads of Agreement for Tourism in National Parks, the English Tourist Board and Countryside Commission sought a location for a pilot project to manage traffic levels.
- An early joint initiative in Borrowdale failed. Here a park and ride scheme was devised but ran into opposition from traders fearful of losing business through high parking charges. There was also a general feeling that car problems had been exaggerated, later confirmed by survey. A more coordinated, less piecemeal approach was needed, embracing local consultation.

The initiative is a joint project between Cumbria County Council, the National Park Authority, Countryside Commission and the English Tourist Board and Cumbria Tourist Board.

The objectives in the initial strategy were to:
- reduce periodic traffic congestion and parking congestion;
- offer alternative modes of transport to the car;
- reduce the impact of increasing levels of traffic on the countryside;
- tailor traffic to the availability of the existing road;
- ensure that the National Park remains accessible for quiet enjoyment, irrespective of income or disability;
- enable the local community to proceed with its normal business.

Organisation and funding

The initiative is steered by a group of senior officers from the four sponsoring bodies, supported by a working group of executive officers. An Advisory Group at member level meets occasionally.

Some of the work is coordinated through a Public Transport Action Group (involving local authority officers, transport operators and recreation interests) and a Highways Action Group (involving county and district technical officers).

Although there are many groups, this structure appears to work. It provides a forum in which tourism and conservation concerns can strike a balance. Working alongside organisations involved with visitors helps the technical officers to think strategically. Highways and transport officers at a county level are better able to coordinate their work with officers at a district level who are concerned with parking and infrastructure.

The Initiative has a part time coordinator and a project officer currently seconded on a temporary basis from the County Council.

Financial summary:

Average annual core budget: £40,000

Income:	Countryside Commission	35%
	English Tourist Board	25%
	Cumbria County Council	20%
	National Park	20%
Expenditure:	Salaries and admin	77%
	Expenditure	23%

Individual projects are funded from outside budgets. In 1995 the County Highway Authority is putting in an extra £75,000 and the National Park £20,000.

Approach

Traffic management used to be piecemeal, making small adjustments to accommodate demand and otherwise relying on the self-regulating effect of congestion. This initiative seeks a more active, comprehensive approach involving demand management, to influence how people travel, and resource management, to improve actual traffic conditions.

The Initiative works with local people and visitors through:

- Close community liaison. Projects are only progressed where local people have identified and accepted the need. Sometimes communities come to the Initiative, sometimes vice versa.
- Trying to influence visitor behaviour through information and putting over the environmental arguments in favour of alternative transport or means of access.
- Using the Action Groups to co-ordinate the views of different agencies.

Action flowing from the strategy covers a whole range of topics relating to roads, traffic, transport and access. Elements include: redesignation of roads within a complete new hierarchy; a coordinated public transport network; car park management and park and ride; schemes to meet the specific needs of different kinds of visitor such as fell walkers and non-car users; and information and publicity.

Initiatives

Road hierarchy

It was felt that the current roads classification did not reflect the ability to accommodate traffic, giving the wrong impression to motorists. A consultation report has reconsidered all the roads in the Park, including feeder roads, according to their type and strategic importance. A seven-layer hierarchy has been put forward, with design and traffic control standards (eg speed limits, weight limits) identified for each. A 40 mph limit throughout the Park is proposed for all but Trunk roads. Many minor roads could be downgraded, with a new category of 'Lakeland Lane' which would be signed to take 'no vehicles except for access'. Special consideration will be given to the needs of walkers, cyclists and riders using roads. The proposals, in a consultation document, have been widely distributed throughout the Lake District, and public meetings have been held (see box on page 29).

Public transport services

A draft strategic network plan has been produced for public transport across the area. Initially this showed target levels of service on different routes, but it was felt that this was too detailed as each route would need a realistic assessment according to resources available and the reaction of transport operators.

Work continues to integrate rail, bus and lake steamer transport. A comprehensive travel card embracing all modes of transport is being pursued, following some local success.

Ideas to make public transport services more appealing to visitors have been pursued or discussed, including introducing more guided commentaries on buses, improving the visibility of bus stops, lake jetty renovation, and integrated tours by public transport.

Integrating all forms of Lake District transport. © *Mike Williams/ CC.*

Information delivery

A full colour fold out public transport map was produced early on. 50,000 copies were printed, with distribution via tourist information centres and transport outlets, equally within and outside the area. It shows transport routes clearly but has no timetables or suggested itineraries and little information about the operators, and so is not immediately usable. The map is popular with tourist information centres and has gained media coverage. A lack of monitoring has been rectified in the 1995 edition through the use of an insert. The cost of £8,000 was funded by local authorities, the Countryside Commission and private operators.

A report of public transport timetables was also produced – 5,000 copies saleable at £1. It has proved very difficult to distribute through retailers and tourist information centres. It is now believed that such information should be free. The free newspaper from Stagecoach, the main bus company, has wide distribution and an option may be to include coverage of other services.

Another initiative is improving road signing particularly where traffic restrictions are imposed. These will have a common style and will explain the reasons to motorists, to encourage their support and compliance.

Tailoring services to national park users' needs

The Initiative has worked imaginatively to promote the use of public transport to fell walkers. A 'linear fell-walks' leaflet has been produced setting out 20 walking routes with return links by bus or boat. A simple three colour leaflet, with clear practical information, it is distributed by tourist information centres and other outlets and has generated much public interest. There has been no direct monitoring but evidence of the popularity of linear walking is clear from comparative passenger numbers on the various legs of the Ullswater steamers.

A special colour poster has been produced listing the numbers of taxi services throughout the Lake District, for display in tourist information centres, phone boxes, and accommodation. This is seen as an important complement to the promotion of other forms of public transport – taxis offer a failsafe 'get you home' service for walkers fearful of missing the last bus.

Local initiatives

A number of individual local schemes have been progressed, subject to identified need, local support, cost and achievability. They include:

- Restricting on-road car parking .
- Making roads access only.
- Village traffic calming schemes.
- Bus priority lane to the Windermere ferry.
- Cattle grids and speed limits on open common land.
- Improved bus services in some valleys.
- Village schemes for parking, traffic management and environmental improvement.

In Grasmere, for example, traffic restrictions, improved coach parking and a link between the bus operators and the main attractions, have been introduced.

Consensus is not always easy. In Elterwater, the tourist board is concerned that traffic problems may have been exaggerated, that commercial interests have not been reflected and that off-road parking should be provided to compensate for loss of on-road spaces. In some places, concerns about loss of trade have been met by agreeing signs towards commercial premises. In Bowness, car park signing has been part-funded by the private sector.

The future

Considerable activity has been identified which will need to be implemented.

Funding is being sought to take the initiative forward beyond 1996, but core funding may be difficult to secure. If the County Council takes an increasing role, the partnership approach needs to continue. Dedicated staff may still be needed to act as a focus.

A future package bid for funding from the Department of Transport (DoT) is being pursued. The presence of a comprehensive strategy is increasingly necessary to gain DoT support.

Assessment

This is a major project seeking to tackle a range of important structural issues in traffic and transport rather than just tinkering with a number of small ideas. The combination of pursuing a strategic framework for the whole Park, while also stimulating a number of practical local initiatives, is a particular strength. It is unrealistic to see this as a three year project given its ambitious nature. A critical issue will be securing agreement to local action and funds to implement the many ideas identified.

The Initiative has been controversial. There is debate even between the participating agencies about the extent of the traffic problems and the responses required. Cumbria Tourist Board, for example, has expressed concern about the demand management approach and the scope of some of the control measures put forward, for instance access restrictions in the road hierarchy proposals. The global as well as local arguments for reducing car use could be more precisely identified. At present, the strategy is broad based.

The tourism industry is seen as a key respondent to the extensive consultation exercise undertaken by the Initiative. Industry concerns will need to be properly addressed by the final strategy.

Marketing and publicity could be more effective and better resourced, including campaigns in points of origin such as Manchester as well as in the Lake District itself.

Particular achievements

- Preparing a comprehensive framework which seeks to tackle traffic management and transport opportunities in an integrated way.
- Creating fora for different interests to work together. In particular, helping transport operators work more effectively with others.
- Striking a good balance between a park-wide strategy and proposed local action.
- Creative initiatives in linking public transport with specific recreation needs in the park.

Some lessons and pointers

- Projects can achieve more by enabling rather than doing. This Initiative has been able to pursue an ambitious programme because its approach is to alter the priorities and activities of the main agencies, rather than working alone with limited resources.
- Be sure about delivery and take up of print before production. The difficulty of distributing the timetable report has lessons for others. More consideration is needed of the best way to present and deliver timetable information.
- Consult carefully with all stakeholders, and really understand the scale and nature of the problem, before proceeding with traffic and transport schemes. The experience from the Borrowdale scheme shows the importance of this.

The South Devon Green Tourism Initiative — Greening tourism business

A national pilot study to test techniques of encouraging tourism businesses to adopt environmentally sound practices

Location:	South Devon
Partners:	Countryside Commission, English Tourist Board, Rural Development Commission, West Country Tourist Board, Devon County Council, South Hams District Council, Torbay Borough Council, Plymouth City Council, Dartington Hall Trust, Plymouth Marketing Bureau.
Structure:	Steering group; full time project officer
Timescale:	1993–1994
Core funding:	£41,000 annual average.

Points of interest:
- Putting over green messages for businesses with Green Audit Kit.
- Using networks to spread interest amongst private sector operators.
- Take up and response from private sector.
- Training and advice for businesses.
- Raising money for conservation

Context

South Devon is a one of the most popular destinations for tourism in the UK. The project area included a major seaside resort (Torbay), a sizeable city (Plymouth) and a very attractive rural district which includes part of a National Park and a long stretch of Heritage Coast (South Hams). It was critical for the Initiative to establish the fact that 'green tourism' was not the same as 'rural tourism', but was about environmentally sensitive tourism irrespective of location.

Origin and objectives

This initiative stems from Government Task Force report *Tourism and the environment – Maintaining The Balance*, and the subsequent publication *The green light – A guide to sustainable tourism*. The latter document was particularly concerned with the need to encourage the tourism industry to adopt environmentally sound practices. The English Tourist Board/Countryside Commission/Rural Development Commission were keen to fund a national pilot project to demonstrate

how this might be achieved on the ground. Following a national invitation for bids the West Country Tourist Board and their partners in South Devon were chosen as a project location.

The original aim of the project brief was: 'To demonstrate and encourage the concept of sustainable tourism through the development, operation and promotion of tourism by operators, in a manner which benefits the local economy at the same time as protecting and enhancing the environment'.

Early on in the project it was decided to concentrate effort on seeking ways to influence tourism businesses.

Organisation and funding

A steering group of officers from the funding partners has overseen the initiative, meeting four times a year. Political commitment from the local authorities was secured through the relevant officers.

The initiative has been carried out by a single full time project manager, based in a local office provided by Dartington Hall Trust. Line management was through the West Country Tourist Board, which played an important role in bringing the funding partners together and keeping the initiative going.

Initially the initiative was set to run for only one year. This was quickly recognised as being far too short and funding was established for a second year.

Financial summary:		
Average annual core budget:		£41,000
Income:	English Tourist Board	25%
	Countryside Commission	25%
	Rural Development Commission	25%
	Local authorities	25%
Also help in kind from the West Country Tourist Board and Dartington Hall Trust		
Expenditure:	Salary and overheads	58%
	Projects	42%

Approach

The original brief called for the development of a do-it-yourself environmental audit manual for tourism enterprises. The Initiative therefore centred around producing *The Green Audit Kit* and then promoting it to enterprises across the area.

A few additional activities have been pursed, but only where they have a bearing on private sector businesses.

Monitoring has been an important part of the Initiative. The take up of the kit was accurately recorded against initial targets, and this was regularly reported to the steering group. An independent assessment of the kit, based on research amongst users, was separately funded by the agencies, and fed back into the Initiative.

Initiatives

Producing the kit

The project manager spent the first nine months writing the kit. This was done in close consultation with local businesses, testing out ideas and producing drafts. The kit was prepared as a loose leaf folder so that pages could be photocopied, people could add their own bits and updates could be bound in to reflect technical changes. Separate sections covered: energy, transport, purchasing, waste, health and conserving the local environment. Each section had: an information sheet, explaining the issues and how to tackle them; an audit sheet, for users to fill in to record what they had done; and an action sheet, which showed through symbols the relative benefits of different actions in terms of overheads, costs, payback and environmental benefits.

Special attention was paid to the design of the kit. A bold front cover and use of colours and graphics inside was found to be particularly successful in attracting attention, arousing interest and encouraging its use. The kit was priced modestly at £3.50; subsequent research suggested that this could have been higher.

Environmental consultants commissioned to evaluate the kit found a high level of satisfaction amongst purchasers, but concluded that it should have been structured in a more progressive way.

Promoting use of the kit

Mail shots proved almost totally ineffective. It was found that a personal approach was necessary to explain the purpose of the kit and to let people hear what others were doing.

Targeting key individuals and working through existing business networks proved very successful. Through direct contact or initial presentations a small number of enterprises in each area took up the kit enthusiastically and the project manager kept in close touch with them. These operators were then able to report back to their peers in their local accommodation groups or tourism associations. This was particularly effective where these individuals were already respected and successful entrepreneurs in their areas. Local authorities were helpful with initial contacts and became more enthusiastic when they could see respected commercial operators getting involved.

An initial target of 90 kits sold was soon exceeded. By the end of the second year, 189 businesses were participating in the initiative. Of those enterprises who purchased kits, half had put them to use through doing their own simple audits, and of these a quarter had turned them into action.

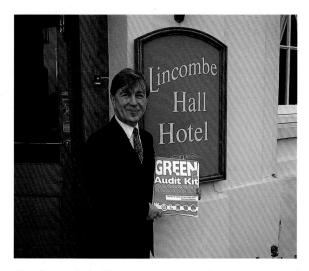

The Green Audit Kit won commitment from managers and owners. © South Devon Green Tourism Initiative.

Feedback on enterprise response

Early research amongst tourism businesses identified a high degree of personal interest in green practices, but most did not see this as a high business priority and were vague about issues such as transport and local conservation. Many did not think the subject would be of much interest to their visitors, and did not realise that it could save them money. It was concluded that if enterprises were given the facts and clearly shown what to do, many would respond.

The project manager found that the spark which really caught their attention was the potential costs savings. Many were also inspired by the need to care for their immediate local environment. Few went into the process in order to gain a marketing advantage, which was fortunate as the Initiative concluded that the market response to a 'green' enterprise is still not proven and requires further research.

Overall action taken by enterprises has been quite practical and varied covering both technical changes and better communication with guests. Care with wording was found to be critical, otherwise visitors could be put off (see box on page 46).

An award scheme

Merit awards were given to enterprises which submitted an environmental plan for the following year and had started to make progress. Rather than measure attainment it rewarded intention, which was felt to be the best way to encourage enterprises who were starting from scratch. 30 merits were awarded. The main weakness with this approach is that merit holders can all be at completely different levels, meaning nothing tangible to the consumer. A scheme based on reaching recognisable step might have more impact and be clearer to customers.

Advice and training

The project manager was able to give back up advice to kit users but was seldom called upon to do so. The Initiative concluded that it would be valuable to have:

- initial training sessions, especially if delivered to small groups working together to apply the kit;
- some local point of contact to iron out difficulties and identify sources of further information.

A 'countryside awareness day' was held for enterprises to draw their attention to local environmental issues which might be of interest to them and their visitors. Talks were given by the Devon Wildlife Trust and local authority officers. A marketing expert gave advice on using green themes in communicating with visitors. Part of the day involved a walk round a local nature reserve. This hands-on experience, where participants were actually looking at things on the ground, was considered to be essential in generating interest. Although attendance was quite low, the day was deemed to be a success in building bridges and providing practical ideas.

Raising funds for conservation

Two alternative ways for businesses to raise conservation funds from visitors were tested. The first entailed selling a set of discount offers made available by enterprises (see box on page 37). The second involves a voluntary levy administered through 15 hotels in the Dartmouth area, who have been receptive to the idea owing to their established relationship with the Initiative.

The future

The approach is being taken forward in South Devon by the local authorities. A national version of the kit is being prepared for launch in 1995 in the light of the evaluation and experience gained through the Initiative.

Assessment

The Initiative has successfully demonstrated that good self-help materials, carefully promoted, can have an impact on enterprises, and has lead to ongoing activity at both a local and a national level. Compared with many other projects, it benefited from the focus of a specific task to which it could devote its full attention. It was also fortunate in promoting something which was completely new and could be easily monitored.

Particular achievements

- The quality and appearance of the kit, which comes over as both authoritative and lively.
- The healthy take up of the kit and the use made of it, which exceeded initial expectations.
- Skilful working with individuals and networks to spread interest.

Some lessons and pointers

- Tourism enterprises are responsive to green concepts, providing the benefits are carefully spelt out to them and they are shown how they might respond.
- Find ways of influencing existing trade groups or associations, so they can exert peer pressure on members. It would have been far too time consuming for the Initiative to have promoted its ideas on an individual basis.
- Pay particular attention to wording when putting over green messages to visitors, especially when seeking to influence their behaviour.
- It is worth investing in good design and especially a striking cover, if you want major print items to be influential.
- Keep administration and fund raising separate from project work. The West Country Tourist Board played an invaluable role in this, releasing the project manager to concentrate on implementation.

The Settle and Carlisle Railway Development Company — Rallying around a railway

A project which uses the profile of the Settle – Carlisle railway to stimulate tourism and economic development along an isolated rural corridor, promoting the use of the line to help safeguard its future.

Location:	72 mile corridor from Settle, North Yorkshire to Carlisle, Cumbria
Partners:	English Tourist Board, Rural Development Commission, Cumbria Tourist Board, Yorkshire and Humberside Tourist Board, various local authorities, British Nuclear Fuels Ltd., Regional Railways, private sector, private individuals.
Structure:	Company limited by guarantee, with a board of directors and an ad hoc management group
Timescale:	3 years, 1992–1995. Future funding being sought.
Core funding:	£50,000 annual average.

Points of interest:
- Integrated marketing and site development work.
- Coordination of marketing activity between agencies.
- Direct promotion of tour programmes using public transport.
- Involvement of local education authorities in interpretation to schools.
- Catalytic role for major economic development projects.

Context

The Settle – Carlisle railway line, part of the national rail network, is one of the most scenically attractive routes in Britain. The area it serves are remote, with many of the problems of rural isolation. The line lies on the margins of three regions and the local communities tend to feel passed by in terms of tourism, economic development and political priority. Yet the Settle – Carlisle line has become well known nationally and gives the area an image to build upon.

Origins and objectives

In the 1980s the line was threatened with closure. A campaign to save it was mounted by voluntary pressure groups and local authorities, which achieved considerable publicity. In 1989 the Government gave the line a reprieve, but required that all agencies should work together to secure its long term future and benefit the communities around it. This led to the formation of the Settle and Carlisle Railway Development Company.

The Company's mission is: 'To promote and coordinate appropriate developments in the corridor of the railway, to bring both economic and community benefits to the region, and to safeguard the future of the railway'.

The Company is concerned with economic development, not just with tourism. Its activities embrace stimulating inward investment, site development along the line, information and marketing. With hindsight, its initial aims were too broad and ambitious, and in the first year it suffered from a lack of focus.

Organisation and funding

The Company is limited by Guarantee. A Board of Directors meets three times a year, comprising named individuals from the local authorities, Rural Development Commission, Cumbria Tourist Board, Cumbria Training Enterprise Council plus four directors from the private sector.

Limited company status allowed total independence from any one organisation and enables public and private interests and expertise to come together. This has been a mixed blessing. It has enabled a flexible approach and an ability to receive funding directly into the Company, yet legal requirements make it time consuming to set up and administer.

The Company works with a number of voluntary groups which had been formed to preserve and secure the line, including the Settle and Carlisle Railway Business Liaison Group, which brings together small local enterprises, and Friends of the Settle and Carlisle Line, which coordinates local enthusiasts. Recently a Marketing Group has been formed which includes local authority tourism staff, tourist boards, and the above two groups, which has been seen as essential for coordinating and focusing marketing.

The functions of the Company are carried out by a full time manager and a part time assistant, based in an office in Settle.

Financial summary:

Average annual core funding:		£50,000
Income:	Rural Development Commission	42%
	Local authorities	44%
	British Nuclear Fuels Limited	14%
	other small sponsors	
Expenditure:	Salaries and administration	63%
	Projects	37%

The Company has been particularly successful in raising help in kind for initiatives.

Approach

In 1993, a Tourism Strategy was prepared for the Company which formed the basis of the tourism initiatives. It identified:

- three target markets: day visitors, short breaks and educational groups;
- three key development sites: Hellifield, Appleby and Carlisle; and
- three marketing objectives: more use of the line; getting people out of the trains to spend money locally (initial research showed that the majority travelled the full distance and returned); and raising the profile of the area.

The Strategy refers to green tourism principles and recognises that tourism supported by the Company needs to be both economically and environmentally sustainable.

Initial market research was undertaken at the start of the project to establish who was using the line. A further survey will shortly be undertaken to measure visitor reactions and experiences. This will assist in assessment of the impact of the project. Some monitoring of uptake of individual initiatives has also occurred.

The approach has been to pursue physical development and marketing initiatives in parallel, with each supporting the other.

Initiatives undertaken

Underpinning site development

Development work has focused around the three sites identified in the strategy. Projects at Hellifield and Appleby stations have been the subject of successful Single Regeneration Budget bids put together by the Company and partners.

Hellifield is strategically located at a junction on the line. The fine Victorian station buildings were restored at an earlier stage. The Company has identified entrepreneurs who propose to create an interpretation centre and visitor attraction there, together with a steam train operation. A feasibility study has been undertaken and job creation is estimated at 100. At Appleby, an attraction centred on rolling stock restoration has been devised, which may be managed by the Company.

Tourism provides a justification for restoring the Victorian station at Hellifield. © The Settle–Carlisle Railway Development Company.

Information and marketing

An early initiative was the production of a full colour map and guide to the line, printed in large quantities for free distribution via tourist information centres and British Rail outlets. This has been useful in creating a visual identity and image for the area.

An attractive yet simple two colour brochure featuring 28 accommodation establishments offering two–three night breaks between September 1994 and May 1995 was produced (10,000 copies). It was promoted through tourist information centres, local authorities and a small ad. campaign. Many public enquiries have been received but a survey suggests that conversion to booking has been very low. The breaks are not directly linked to travel by rail, but contain a small discount offer for travel on the line itself. For 1995, the rail discount is being more attractive.

Research has determined which coach companies are bringing groups to the railway corridor and these have been individually targeted. The Company has created a special guided tour programme in partnership with a bus operator and Regional Railways. The programme has been successfully marketed in the Lake District and is being expanded. This is a good example of targeted, creative marketing opening opportunities for private sector partnership (see box on page 30).

The potential for walking routes using the railway was identified by the Marketing Group, to promote alongside short breaks. A publication is being produced by Cumbria County Council.

Schools have been targeted for educational reasons, to promote off-season tourism, and generate future return business. Teachers were seconded to prepare a high quality resource pack, promoted to schools across northern England.

The future

Core funding from the national agencies ended in 1995. More limited funding from the local authorities has been assembled to carry the Company on for at least one more year. Further resources will be earned from consultancy and marketing work. The Marketing Group will be ongoing, as a force for future coordination.

Assessment

The Company got off to a slow start, hampered by the bureaucracy of setting up a Company Limited by Guarantee and by a lack of priorities. It became important to fix on a small number of projects which could be delivered.

The Company has succeeded in raising the profile of the area amongst the local authorities and public sector agencies. It is no longer seen as marginal, and structures have been formed for the relevant agencies to work together in future. In particular, Regional Railways was brought in as a partner. Rail privatisation has caused uncertainty but may offer future opportunities through Rail Track seeking maximum commercial use of the line.

As a tourism initiative centred around rail use and supporting local communities the Company has followed sustainable principles. However, these should have been built into the objectives at an early stage.

The Company is hampered through having little influence over the railway itself.

Not much has been done actually to improve the visitor experience. Interpretation of the line, stations and surrounding communities is poor. This will need to be addressed if line is to be sustained as a credible visitor attraction.

Particular achievement

- Helping to pioneer appropriate site development work, to create a more permanent product, alongside a range of marketing activities.
- Establishing a marketing group of relevant interests to focus their activity on the line, and feeding opportunities to this group.
- Working alongside a commercial operator to establish and promote a marketing product which meets the objectives of the Company.
- Creating and educational and interpretative resource.

Some lessons and pointers

- Ensure that the initial objectives are well focused and clear and capable of being achieved within resources.
- Establishing a Company Limited by Guarantee has both advantages and disadvantages. The more proactive and commercial approach of this project may partly reflect the fact that it is an independent company. However, probably for a short term project this creates unnecessary legal and administrative work.
- It is difficult to create much impact with separate, low budget short break campaigns.
- Specific measurable benefits can be obtained in promoting to groups and working alongside commercial operators.

The Norfolk Coast Project — Comprehensive visitor management

This project is a careful example of a systematic approach to visitor management from strategy, action programme to implementation.

Location: The north coast of Norfolk

Partners: Countryside Commission, Norfolk County Council, North Norfolk District Council, Kings Lynn and West Norfolk Borough Council.

Structure: Full time project team with officer working group and advisory panel.

Timescale: 1991–1998.

Core funding: £82,000 annual average.

Points of interest:
- Preparation of visitor management strategy after extensive consultation.
- Zoning of area to reflect ecological sensitivity and visitor use.
- Testing and disseminating practical visitor management techniques.
- Comprehensive action programme being pursued.

Context

The Norfolk Coast Area of Outstanding Natural Beauty extends to some 451 sq km, including 70 km of coastline, mostly designated Heritage Coast. This coast is the primary feature of the area including expanses of salt marsh, together with dunes and sand and shingle beaches. The Area of Outstanding Natural Beauty contains wetlands and bird habitats of international importance. Inland there are attractive woodlands and farmland, including a chalk ridge and heathland. There are a number of attractive small towns and villages. Tourism is traditional in the area, but there is increasing concern about visitor impact and congestion, especially on the narrow coast road and on some popular coastal sites important for wildlife.

Origin and objectives

Conservation and management work has taken place for some time. An earlier Heritage Coast initiative tackled some of these issues, but with no officer to make things happen. The Norfolk Coast Project stemmed from:
- local concern about increasing visitor pressure, especially amongst the local authorities and conservation bodies;
- national and regional interest in the concept of green or sustainable tourism.

A project emerged to bring these two strands together. There was some uncertainly as to whether this was essentially a 'sustainable tourism' project or a coastal management project. It was resolved as an Area of Outstanding Natural Beauty project focusing on visitor management.

Local authorities initially saw tourism from a planning perspective. It was quickly realised that marketing and information issues should be embraced, resulting in the involvement of the local authority tourism officers.

In 1992, objectives were not very clear; by 1994 they were represented as:
- To ensure use of the area is sustainable, that it does not destroy its natural beauty, and that future generations have the same opportunity to enjoy and benefit from it.
- To preserve and enhance the beauty of the Norfolk Coast.
- To facilitate and enhance the public's enjoyment, understanding and appreciation of the area.
- To promote sustainable forms of social and economic development that conserve and enhance the area's natural beauty.

Organisation and funding

There is a project officer and assistant, part time administrator and a part time officer who carries out access work. The team works from an independent office in the centre of the Area of Outstanding Natural Beauty .

An Officer Working Group, comprises the Countryside Commission, Norfolk County Council, North Norfolk District and West Norfolk Borough Councils and two district councils, as funders, together with the East Anglia Tourist Board, Eastern Sports Council, Rural Development Commission and representatives from conservation bodies, landowning interests and the local community.

A smaller informal group of the funding agencies also exists. There is also an advisory panel involving local authority members, to provide political and policy context.

Community representation now includes five parishioners following disquiet that the project was too dominated by conservation interests. The local tourism industry is not directly represented, and liaison with this sector has not been easy.

Financial summary:		
Average annual core budget		£82,000
Income:	Countryside Commission	50%
	Norfolk County Council	25%
	North Norfolk District	12.5%
	King's Lynn and West	
	Norfolk District Councils	12.5%
Expenditure:	Staff/admin	60%
	Projects	40%

The project has secured additional resources beyond the core budget: for example, from the Rural Development Commission towards the visitor newspaper and public transport services.

Approach

The project focus is visitor management. A visitor management strategy was prepared; a painstaking exercise involving a considerable amount of local consultation. A subsequent Action Plan featured 43 tasks.

To implement the plan, the project seeks to stimulate and prioritise the work of others. The Officer Working Group is responsible for this, and lead officers are identified from the various authorities to take tasks forward. Responsibility is shown in the Action Plan, which is updated to show progress and identify next steps.

The project also influences other strategies and policies including the district council tourism strategies and individual local plans. The Action Plan is reflected in the Rural Development Commission's Rural Development Programme for the area.

Attractive villages close to coastal nature reserves call for sound visitor management. © Norfolk Coast Project.

Initiatives undertaken

Visitor Management Strategy

The Visitor Management Strategy was prepared carefully to reflect local opinion. Four working groups covered nature conservation, landscape, recreation, and socio-economic issues. This structure enabled additional local interests to contribute.

Two surveys were undertaken to inform this work:
- A questionnaire to 11,000 local households, backed up by a newsletter. Only 350 responses were received, partly due to distribution problems.
- A 'day diary' questionnaire for visitors, to record profiles, activities, spending etc. These were distributed at car parks, attractions and tourist information centres. 300 were returned.

Despite the low response, some helpful insights were obtained.

The initial draft strategy contained 89 policies. This was far too many to guide action effectively, so the strategy was simplified down to 45 policies. Topics included local communities and the local economy, traffic and transport, landscape and archaeology, habitats and wildlife, pollution, information and interpretation, recreation and tourism.

The exercise took almost two years to complete. This was perhaps too long, and the project risked being seen as a talking shop, with nothing to show. However, local involvement and consensus building through the working groups was a strength. The process was considered to be as important as the end product.

Zoning policy

Integral with the Strategy, a zoning exercise was undertaken. Six zones were identified, taking account of habitat sensitivity and visitor use, ranging from very sensitive areas already under pressure, to areas of opportunity for more access and facilities in keeping with the environment of the Area of Outstanding Natural Beauty. Zoning decisions were taken on the basis of feedback on visitor 'incidents' from different sites and on informed professional judgement. A map was prepared showing the different zones, and is used to prioritise management resources and guide planning decisions. Consideration is being given to further publicity for the zone map and the concept of varying sensitivity, possibly via a leaflet (see box on page 17).

Traffic and transport

The project has encouraged Norfolk County Council to undertake a comprehensive traffic and transport study for the Area of Outstanding Natural Beauty. This has suffered from lack of time and resources, and small studies on demand management, cycling and parking may be pursued instead.

A public transport map, usefully incorporating timetables, has been distributed widely, including to tourism enterprises. The project has helped to develop a new Sunday Explorer bus service, subsidised by the County Council. In the second year, half the costs of the subsidy were met through increased commercial returns and passenger use is continuing to increase.

Opportunities for walks using the bus have been promoted in the Project's newspaper. The zoning policy has guided this work, based on the principle of encouraging car borne visitors to park in the more robust zones and use public transport to access more fragile areas. However, there are no surveys to show the effectiveness of this.

Landscape and site management

Design guidelines have been published to improve the sensitivity of small structures in the landscape, such as bird hides which can easily be obtrusive.

Problems with off-road vehicle use have been tackled. Individual grants given for visitor management work on sites (such as board walks) have been prioritised according to the zoning policy. Some surveys of wildlife have been grant aided to monitor the effect of visitor impact. The project has played an important role in bringing together the local wardens from the various conservation organisations to tackle common issues.

A particularly successful exercise has been carried out on beach visitor management. A researcher was employed for six months to undertake a visitor survey and observe visitor behaviour at a sensitive beach site, testing out different information methods and physical management techniques. For example, trying out different wording on signs and observing whether they were read, and experimenting with leaflet designs and innovative dog management techniques. The results were written up in a *Visitor Management Handbook* for all the local wardens throughout the Area of Outstanding Natural Beauty, which has been enthusiastically received, and used in visitor leaflets.

Visitor codes

Emphasis has been placed on publicising codes of behaviour for visitors. A general code was drawn up covering use of cars and transport, how to avoid disturbing wildlife, the benefits of shopping locally etc. This has been inserted in local holiday guides as well as in the project's own material. The effect of this is hard to monitor. Codes for local reserves have been developed and recreation-specific codes considered.

The Coast Guardian newspaper

A visitor newspaper has been produced for distribution only within the local area, to get messages across to existing visitors but not to draw others to the coast. The Norfolk Coast Guardian combines articles on local themes and conservation with information on places to visit (according to zoning guidance), an events guide, public transport promotion and conservation messages. Print runs were doubled in the second year to 50,000. In 1995 the paper was part funded by the project, with 50 per cent coming from advertising and 25 per cent from a Rural Development Commission grant. To monitor impact, the 1995 edition has a prize competition to stimulate feedback. The paper has been well received and has proved an excellent medium for promoting the project's approach and communicating with tourism operators.

Other initiatives

Other schemes include research into the potential for a local tourism heritage trust and the promotion of local traditions and products. A survey of food producers and outlets is proposed. Others plans include an interpretation strategy and projects and a cycle tourism initiative.

The future

The current priority is to pursue practical initiatives to implement the visitor management action plan. In future a general management strategy for the Area of Outstanding Natural Beauty will be prepared. Decisions will need to be taken on how far to get involved in additional socio-economic work. The project will be reviewed in 1997–1998.

Assessment

A key feature has been the strategy and action programme. The particular strength has been that is has

- focused exclusively on visitor management, though interpreting this quite broadly;
- been an internal exercise and an integral part of the project.

Getting things done through others, and showing clear responsibilities through the action plan, should enable the project to create impact over time. However, commitment needs maintaining by all partners.

The length of time taken to prepare the strategy is a possible weakness, though it probably created a stronger sense of local ownership and agreement. Action can now be undertaken from a firm base.

More might have been done to involve the local tourism industry and to encourage their commitment to suitable tourism and conservation. The local authority tourism officers should have been seen as integral partners from the start.

Much of the work has been hard to quantify and monitor, and greater attempts need to be made to monitor impacts in the future.

Particular achievements

- Generally raising the profile of the Area of Outstanding Natural Beauty.
- Bringing different interests together with a practical task of producing a strategy which they could all share.
- A dynamic action programme, capable of being rolled forward into the future.
- Creative practical research on beach management, leading to effective dissemination of lessons learnt.
- Simple mechanisms for distributing information to visitors, especially through the visitor newspaper.

Some lessons and pointers

- A structure for stimulating and supporting action by others rather than trying to do it all within the project, can be valuable.
- A carefully constructed strategy, involving local people and diverse interests, can form a good basis for visitor management work.
- Zoning and mapping can be used effectively as a way of summarising impacts and issues clearly, which different interests can understand.

The Nightingale Project — Promoting Kent's wildlife

A project which has promoted Kent's wildlife as a resource for tourism.

Location:	Kent
Partners:	Countryside Commission, English Nature, South East Tourist Board, Kent County Council, Kent Trust for Nature Conservation, National Trust.
Timescale:	October 1991 – October 1994
Core funding:	£47,000 annual average.

Points of interest:
- Themed approach concentrating on nature conservation.
- Attractive brochures and literature.
- Comprehensive monitoring.

Context

Kent is an attractive county with a wide range of different habitats and associated wildlife ranging from the waders and wildfowl of the North Kent Marshes to the orchids and butterflies of the North Downs. The county is readily accessible to day visitors from London and is also the main gateway to continental Europe through the Channel Ports and Tunnel.

Origins and objectives

This project evolved out of discussions between Kent Trust for Nature Conservation and the Economic Development Department of Kent County Council about the funding of a new visitor centre and offices for the Trust.

The Nightingale Project was devised as a way of strengthening links between nature conservation and economic development. The Trust saw this as a way of strengthening support for nature conservation. Kent County Council wanted to make better use of Kent's natural environment to attract tourism and were also looking for ways to counter Kent's image as an area suffering from congestion and major infrastructure projects.

The aim of the Nightingale Project was 'to promote the wildlife of Kent as a sensitively marketed tourist attraction... and make the wildlife of the County more accessible to, and understandable by, tourists'.

Four main areas of work were identified at the outset of the project:
- Marketing existing wildlife resources.
- Advising wildlife attractions and sites on developing new projects.
- Coordinating and marketing events.
- Providing information on wildlife to the public.

Other organisations and agencies with an interest in wildlife conservation and tourism were invited to participate and the project was formally established in October 1991.

Organisation and funding

A steering group was established with officer level representatives from the Trust, Kent County Council (Planning and Economic Development), National Trust, English Nature, Countryside Commission, South East England Tourist Board and RSPB. This group met quarterly and was chaired by the Director of the Trust.

An advisory group with a wider spread of membership was established with the purpose of getting conservation interests behind the project . This met on a six monthly basis and one of the initial ideas was that this group might eventually evolve into a Green Tourism Forum for Kent. In practice the role of the advisory and steering groups became blurred and they were eventually amalgamated.

A full-time project officer was appointed working out of Tyland Barn, with the Trust providing office accommodation and administrative support. Part of the role of the project officer was seen as putting the Tyland Barn visitor centre on the map.

Financial summary:		
Average annual core funding		£47,000 pa
Income:	Kent County Council	56%
	Countryside Commission	11%
	English Nature	20%
	Kent Trust for Nature Conservation	7%
	Other	6%
Expenditure:	Staff/admin	55%
	Projects	45%

Approach

No formal strategy was produced. The project officer drew up a work programme in the light of the project objectives and this was rolled forward on an annual basis. With hindsight a clearer definition of the scope of the project at the outset might have helped resolve difficulties that surfaced later.

Initiatives undertaken

Marketing and information

A key piece of print was a leaflet setting out details of 24 wildlife sites in the county, *Where to see wildlife in Kent* produced as a folded A2 sized colour leaflet. Some 150,000 copies were produced over the course of the project and distributed within the County via tourist information centres, libraries, accommodation establishments and attractions. The leaflet was popular with tourist information centres although the majority of the sites featured were unable to say whether it had had any impact on visitor numbers.

A companion leaflet, *Wildlife activities in Kent*, set out details of trails, guided walks, wildlife and farm attractions, and conservation holidays. 100,000 were printed, (10,000 in French and German) and these were distributed both within and outside the county and used at exhibitions. Again the operators and attractions featured were unable to say how effective the leaflet was at generating business although they agreed to contribute towards a reprint. Coupon responses from the two leaflets were minimal.

An eight page supplement was produced in association with the *Kent Messenger* newspaper publicising Tyland Barn and Kent's wildlife. Some 140,000 copies were distributed in Kent and the exercise was repeated the following year. There was a positive reaction to this with the first supplement generating some 1,850 enquiries including 1,400 entries for a children's competition.

Other pieces of print included leaflets on Tyland Barn and events. Associated activities consisted of regional trade exhibitions, press releases, familiarisation trips and talks to local groups. A national seminar on green tourism was also arranged which attracted widespread interest and stimulated at least one project by a local Parish Council.

Events

The project was responsible for coordinating and publicising a range of events held at Tyland Barn marketed under imaginative titles such as *Bees and all that business* and *Discover the Dormouse at the Mad Hatters Tea Party*. Tyland Barn exceeded its visitor targets.

Development advice

One of the aims of the project was to offer a consultancy and advice service. This was seen as a way of encouraging the upgrading and provision of facilities as well as earning some additional income. A number of projects were visited by the project officer although this proved quite time consuming and relatively little was earned by way of income.

Pond dipping adds interest to a wildlife activity day at Tyland Barn. © Nightingale Project.

Monitoring

Considerable emphasis was placed on monitoring. The aim was to establish a benchmark against which progress and impact of the project could be measured. Initiatives included:

- Site surveys to collect information on the impact of visitors, based on a questionnaire completed by site managers on an annual basis.
- Visitor surveys carried out at wildlife site and other locations in Kent to measure use of sites, awareness of publications etc. This was designed to be undertaken by local college students. A summary report has been produced.
- Monitoring the impact of the various marketing initiatives. In practice this proved difficult to measure.
- A review of the promotional literature in Kent to identify gaps and opportunities for wildlife. The intention was to review this periodically.

Setting up and coordinating the above placed a considerable burden on the project manager's time. Although the intention to monitor impacts was laudable much of this effort was wasted because in the event no resources were forthcoming to continue this work.

Countryside Stewardship Scheme

In 1993, the project was selected as one of seven case-study projects for the Countryside Stewardship Exchange Scheme. As a result a case study of green tourism in the North Kent Marshes was prepared and this later formed the basis of a European Union LIFE bid coordinated by the Trust. This was unfortunately unsuccessful.

The future

Kent County Council had some reservations about the impact of the project on tourism. The project was reviewed in 1993 and it was decided to extend the life of the project and widen its scope At a seminar in 1994, it was suggested that the Nightingale project should coordinate a Green Tourism Partnership embracing a wide range of tourism and conservation interests across Kent.

In practice this didn't happen. The project officer left causing staffing problems. There were concerns about possible overlap with other projects and an attempt to combine the project with other initiatives failed to secure support.

Assessment

This has been an interesting project which has focused on one particular strand of the rural tourism experience. It has strengthened the links between conservation and tourism interests, produced some useful publications and generally raised interest amongst the public. More than most projects it has made a conscious effort to measure visitor impacts and attitudes.

The overall impact of the project, however, has been modest. This is partly because the project officer left before the end of the project and partly because the project deliberately broadened its emphasis from the initial tight focus on wildlife. In the end it rather fizzled out. With hindsight, more stress should perhaps have been placed on measuring the impact of initiatives and less on establishing baseline visitor information. A greater involvement with the local tourism industry might also have strengthened the position of the project.

Particular achievements

- Forging links between tourism and conservation. The project has brought together both tourism and nature conservation interests and demonstrated that both sides can gain by working together.
- Useful publications. A series of well produced and well received leaflets have been produced and distributed in significant numbers.
- Putting the Tyland Barn visitor centre on the map and encouraging interest, particularly amongst Kent residents.

Some lessons and pointers

- It is important to clarify objectives at the outset. There was some tension in this project as a result of the differing objectives of the tourism and the conservation interests. This led to a weakening of the project in its final year which might have been avoided.
- Monitoring is important but needs to be related to the resources available. There is little point in setting up sophisticated monitoring systems which cannot be sustained in the future.
- Feedback is required to win support. Demonstrating that initiatives are achieving results is critically important to maintaining support and commitment.

CASE STUDY PROJECT CONTACTS

Contact names and addresses for each of the projects are given below.

Big Apple — Jackie Denman, Secretary Big Apple Association, Woodcroft, Putley, Ledbury, Herefordshire HR8 2RD.

Birds of the Humber Trust — Hugh Roberts, Humberside County Council, Leisure Services, 5th Floor, Prospect House, Prospect Street, Hull HU2 8PU.

Celebrate the Countryside — Nigel Buckler, West Country Tourist Board, 60 St Davids Hill, Exeter, Devon EX4 4SY.

Country Village Weekend Breaks — David Gorvett, The Cruck House, Eardisley, Herefordshire HR3 6PQ.

Dartmoor Area Tourism Initiative — Ros Love, Dartmoor National Park, Parke, Haytor Road, Bovey Tracey, Devon TQ13 9JQ.

Devon and Cornwall Rail Partnership — Andrew Seedhouse, Project Officer, Faculty of Science, Plymouth University, Drake Circus, Plymouth PL4 8AA.

Lake District Traffic Management — Andy Ryland, Project Officer, Lake District National Park, Meoley Moss, Oxenholme Rd, Kendal LA9 7RL.

Nightingale Project — Pete Raine, Kent Trust for Nature Conservation, Tyland Barn, Sandling, Maidstone, Kent ME14 3BD.

Norfolk Coast Project — Graeme Hayes, Project Officer, 6 Station Road, Wells-next-the-Sea, Norfolk NR23 1AE.

North Pennines Tourism Partnership — Catharine Bowmer, Project Officer, Barclays Bank Chambers, Front Street, Alston, Cumbria CA9 3SE.

North York Moors Regional Routes — Bill Breakwell, North York Moors National Park, The Old Vicarage, Bondgate, Helmsley, York YO6 5BP.

Peak Tourism Partnership — Andrew Keeling, East Midlands Tourist Board, Exchequergate, Lincoln, Lincolnshire LN2 1PZ.

Project Explore — Kaja Sylvest, Project Officer Discovery Centre, Millpool, Looe, Cornwall PL13 2AF.

Purbeck Heritage Project — Alison Turnock, Project Officer, Westport House, Wareham, Dorset BH20 4PP.

Settle and Carlisle Railway Development Company — Hadyn Morris, Cumbria Tourist Board, Ashleigh, Holly Road, Windemere, Cumbria A23 2AQ.

South Devon Green Tourism Initiative — Delwyn Matthews, West Country Tourist Board, 60 St Davids Hill, Exeter, Devon EX4 4SY.

South Somerset District Council — Martin Woods, Tourism Officer, Council Offices, Brympton Way, Yeovil BA20 1PU.

Surrey Hills Visitor Project — John Phillips, Surrey County Council, Tourism Unit, County Hall, Kingston upon Thames, Surrey KT1 2DN.

Tarka Project — Beverley Trowbridge, Project Officer, Tarka Project, Bideford Station, Railway Terrace, Bideford, Devon EX39 4BB.

Wiltshire Downs Project — Sarah Jackson, Project Officer, Kennet District Council, Browfoot, Bath Road, Devises, Wiltshire SN10 2AT.

Yorkshire Dales Food & Craft Trails — Harry Silcock, Rural Development Commission, Spitfire House, Aviator Court, Clifton Moor YO3 4UZ.

ACKNOWLEDGEMENTS

Finally, we are indebted to all those who gave their time and attention to providing us with information, comments and guidance. Particular thanks must go to our steering group for their support and guidance and also to the project officers and managers who have been commendably open and objective in sharing both their successes and their failures with us. The success and achievements of these projects is due in no small way to the hard work, dedication and professionalism of these individuals.

COUNTRYSIDE
COMMISSION

John Dower House
Crescent Place, Cheltenham
Gloucestershire GL50 3RA
Telephone: 01242 521381
Fax: 01242 584270

ISBN 0 86170 464 9
CCP 483
Price £18.00